T0321518

Advance Praise for *Terror in Frankfurt*

"*Terror in Frankfurt* brings the terrorism threat front and center and chronicles, through the eyes of U.S. Air Force Staff Sergeant Trevor Brewer, one of the most terrifying terrorist attacks in U.S. Air Force history."

—George Galdorisi, *New York Times* bestselling author of the Tom Clancy *Op Center* series

"News accounts seldom capture or do true justice to a harrowing incident. It takes far more in-depth study and analysis. Brewer and Reed's *Terror in Frankfurt* is a harrowing must-read for anyone who wants to understand terrorism, the radicalization of assassins, and the roots behind it all. It is a story of Hollywood, news reporting, and culpability across a wide spectrum. But most importantly, it's a tale of bravery and perseverance. Read this today to understand tomorrow."

—James Rollins, #1 *New York Times* bestselling author of *Kingdom of Bones*

TERROR IN FRANKFURT

THE UNTOLD STORY ABOUT ONE OF THE WORST TERRORIST ATTACKS IN U.S. AIR FORCE HISTORY

MASTER SERGEANT
TREVOR D. BREWER
and *New York Times* Bestselling Author
W. CRAIG REED

PERMUTED
PRESS

A PERMUTED PRESS BOOK
ISBN: 978-1-63758-441-5
ISBN (eBook): 978-1-63758-442-2

Terror in Frankfurt:
The Untold Story About One of the Worst Terrorist Attacks in U.S. Air Force History
© 2022 by Trevor D. Brewer and W. Craig Reed
All Rights Reserved

Cover art by Cody Corcoran

Permuted Press, LLC
New York • Nashville
permutedpress.com

Published in the United States of America
1 2 3 4 5 6 7 8 9 10

Also by W. Craig Reed

Status-6
Spies of the Deep
The 7 Secrets of Neuron Leadership
Red November

I would like to dedicate this book to the memory and families of Airman First Class Zachary Cuddeback, Senior Airman Nicholas Alden, and all those who survived this terrible incident.

CONTENTS

AUTHOR'S NOTE

While Trevor Brewer was a member of the U.S. Air Force when this book was printed, this book was not produced as a part of his official duties. The use of military ranks, titles, or photographs in uniform do not imply endorsement of this product by the U.S. Air Force, the Department of Defense, or any agency of the U.S. Government. Brewer's opinions are his own and may not reflect the official position or account of these events contained herein as held or recorded by the U.S. Government. Great care and time was taken to research this event to ensure accuracy, and out of respect for those involved. Names for those involved and a few details pertaining to this event may have been changed to protect identities and certain information pertaining to individuals involved, however, real identities may have previously been exposed by the media.

CHAPTER 1

THE TRIAL

The courtroom slowly filled, and the trial commenced. Three judges strode into the room wearing long, red robes and white wigs with tight curls. One judge seemed young with long, blond hair jutting out beyond his wig. Another older judge had dark brown eyes and a stern jawline. A cavern formed between his eyes as he turned his head and glared at me. My palms moistened. I turned away and glanced about the courtroom. Against one wood-paneled wall, seats held an assortment of observers and witnesses.

A door opened and the defendant, guarded by two German police officers, walked into the room. I stared at the terrorist and felt my hands form fists. I forced myself to let out a slow breath and turned my open palms upward. The defendant sat next to his attorney, and the trial began. One of the judges asked me a question. My attorney leaned over and whispered that the judge wanted me to approach the stand. I stood and walked toward the three judges. My attorney followed and stood by my side. The judge with dark eyes held up a pistol: a Belgian Browning 9mm. My heart raced and my knees buckled. My attorney grabbed my arm. He assured me that I'd be alright, but I knew he was lying. I'd never be alright again.

The judge asked me if I recognized the weapon. I nodded. A German translator told me to verbally say yes. I said yes, I recognized the weapon. The judge asked me to describe what I had witnessed the last time I had seen the pistol. My heart pounded in my chest. For a moment, I was no longer in the courtroom. I could not speak as the terrifying memories filled my head. A boom rattled the bus windows. Someone screamed in agony. The wretched smell of sulfuric gunpowder filled the air.

I raised my head above the seat and saw the rage in the eyes of the assailant as he stared at me from a few feet away. He pointed the barrel of the gun at my head. I focused on the black hole inside the metal cylinder and wondered if it was the last thing I'd ever see.

The man moved the gun closer and screamed, "Allahu Akbar!"

I flinched and blew out a breath as he squeezed the trigger.

CHAPTER 2:

THE IMPETUS

I t's not always cold in Mentor, Ohio, but sometimes it feels that way. The average temperature is around fifty, and when the wind whips across the southern edge of Lake Erie, it gets even colder. I grew up in this small town of only 40,000, often cupping my hands over my nose to keep my face from freezing.

Mentor came to life in the early 1800s in Lake County, Ohio's smallest county, which at one time was known as "the rose capital of the nation" because of an abundance of rosebushes. I remember the sweet smell of those flowers when they bloomed in the spring and covered the outskirts of town with rows of pink and red.

During the summer, when the sun finally came out of hiding, it seemed like half of Mentor's population made a beeline for Headlands Beach State Park, the longest public swimming beach in Ohio. Pudgy, white bodies lined the sand in every direction while burgers and hot dogs roasted on nearby grills.

Mentor is only about twenty miles east of Cleveland, but you'd never know it. Small local shops and aging strip malls line Mentor Avenue, as if imagined from a fifties sitcom. Life was very middle class and hometown America back then. We rode bikes and played baseball in the summer, donned football helmets in the fall, and slipped on ice ponds in the winter. In between all that fun, I squeezed in homework, private viola lessons, school orchestra, and tae kwon do.

I was a small kid, a little undersized, and always felt a bit intimidated around the bigger guys. My parents suggested martial arts, and once I started, I was hooked. I enjoyed mastering the moves and learning how to control my mind and body. I also felt a sense of accomplishment when I became good enough to move up a belt. As an adolescent, I hoped it might also make me popular with the ladies.

I didn't grow up with a silver spoon, but I considered myself lucky. My dad, Donald, had served in the U.S. Navy during the Vietnam War but rarely talked about it. He was a tall and proud man of Welsh descent with green eyes. My mom, Diana, loved to cook, clean, and keep a tidy house. Christina, my oldest sister, was twenty-three and no longer lived at home. Tiffany, my other sibling, acted like a typical seventeen-year-old, experimenting with makeup and besieging mom to buy her the latest rock star outfits.

Our home had three levels, three bedrooms, and two bathrooms. We had a below-ground basement where Tiffany and I played Nintendo video games. During the winter, a large fire crackled in the living room and filled the air with the scent of burning logs. In the summer, we splashed and played with friends in our backyard's above-ground swimming pool and roasted steaks on the grill.

When not in school, at the young age of thirteen, I worked part-time as a busboy at an upscale Italian restaurant called Dino's. The owner, Dino, was a good friend of my uncle, which is how I got hired. Dino was a jovial guy who could flip pizza dough with a practiced flair, but his smile vanished if anyone stepped out of line. He demanded hard work and dedication from his employees. We had to wear uniforms, show up on time, wash our hands, and stay busy. Dino was tough on me but taught me a lot about discipline, accountability, and how to manage my money. My parents had coached me about the value of working hard and taking care of my finances, but Dino gave me the opportunity to apply these lessons on the playing field of life.

During a typical evening dinner, my dad always asked us to bow our heads while he said grace. He often talked about how we were fortunate to be blessed with my mom. He said this with a genuine smile and a sparkle in his eye.

Dad worked as an engineer for the railroad and often traveled out of state. I recall one evening when he let us know he had to take a long trip to Pennsylvania. Tiffany was sad and asked him why he often spent weeks away from home. Dad smiled and said he worked hard because he wanted to provide the best for us, that it was his duty, and when we had our own families, we'd understand.

He then looked at me and said I was the man of the house during his time away from home, and he relied on me to take care of my mother and sister. I swallowed hard and said I understood. I felt a great sense of pride, but also fear, because I didn't want to let him down.

After seeing the look on my face, my dad said that doing what's best for others might not always be easy or what I want, but it was the right thing to do. I remember that moment as if it were yesterday, and I've always tried to live by those words. I also recall the morning of 9/11 as if only a day ago.

That morning, on September 11, 2001, a bright autumn sun peeked through the slat blinds covering the windows of my homeroom class at Memorial Middle School. I sat on a bench in front of a table covered with saws, hammers, and chisels. The scent of fresh cut pine mingled with the pungent smell of lathe oil. I had just finished building a wooden shoe box and grinned as my woodshop teacher nodded approval.

Another teacher burst through the door and rushed into the room. She ran toward the back and turned on a small television set. We were focused on our projects, so none of us were paying much attention. Then someone gasped. Someone else stood up and stepped toward the TV. Another student gaped and pointed.

Slowly, I turned my head toward that TV. My eyes opened wide as I saw massive flames shooting out the side of a tall building in New York. One of the Twin Towers collapsed as plumes of fire and debris shot into the air. Shocked, I strained to hear the voice of the announcer and only caught a few comments. I looked to my teacher for answers, but he remained transfixed on the terrifying scene unfolding before us. Tears ran down his cheeks.

The bell rang. Concerned and confused, I left the room. My friends and I were clueless, and no one provided any answers until after lunch, when I went to my orchestra class. We settled into our seats, picked up our instruments, and studied the music sheets on our stands. We expected our teacher, Mrs. Johnson, to deliver her usual remarks about "finding our musical voice," but she remained silent. Her eyes were red and her cheeks moist. Her lips trembled as she found a chair and motioned for everyone to stop tuning their instruments.

The room fell silent.

Mrs. Johnson cleared her throat. "My usual comments are not important today."

She wiped at a tear and continued. "I have something of greater importance to tell you. So please, just listen. Then, if you have questions, ask them. If there are none, you can return to your homeroom or stay here until the school day ends."

I had never seen Mrs. Johnson this serious or this emotional. I sat up straight and cocked an ear.

"There has been an incident," Mrs. Johnson said. "It happened earlier today in New York City. I don't know all the facts yet, but what I do know is that two airplanes flew into the Twin Towers of the World Trade Center."

I swallowed hard. A violinist dropped her bow and let out a gasp.

"A third plane hit the Pentagon just outside Washington, D.C." Johnson said. "A fourth plane flew over Ohio before it crashed in a field in Pennsylvania. No one knows why this happened, but many people were injured or killed."

One girl in the room started crying. Someone wrapped an arm around her shoulder.

Mrs. Johnson offered a sympathetic nod. "I know this is shocking, and I hope we'll have more answers soon."

A violinist raised her hand. Her blue eyes blinked with confusion and fear. "Are we in danger?"

Mrs. Johnson shook her head. "I don't think so, but there is much we don't know yet. However, I've not heard that we're in danger. I'm sure the authorities would have notified us if we were."

A cellist lifted an unsteady hand, "What should do we do?"

"Talk with your parents when you get home and watch the news with them. I'm certain we'll have answers soon."

A rotund bass player dispensed with raising his hand and said, "I think I'm going to pray."

Mrs. Johnson nodded. "I think that would be a good idea."

We all bowed our heads.

During the silence, vivid images of a crashing tower filled my head. I wanted answers. I wanted to know if it was an accident or an attack. I wanted to know if my family was safe.

I wanted to know if our country was now at war.

Later that day, I learned that United Airlines Flight 93 had flown right over our city before making a U-turn back toward Pennsylvania. That evening, my dad sat us down in the living room. His lips formed a tight line. The somber silence made our home feel like a morgue.

"As I'm sure you heard," Dad said, "terrorists attacked our country today."

I sat up straight and felt adrenaline rush through my veins.

"They hijacked four airplanes," he continued, "and flew two of them into the Twin Towers in New York. Another one hit the Pentagon and the fourth one crashed in a field in Pennsylvania."

My mom brought a hand to her face. My sister started sobbing. Equal measures of fear and anger propelled my heart to full throttle.

"They still don't know who was behind the attack, but the terrorists who hijacked the planes appear to be of Middle Eastern descent."

"Muslims?" I said.

Dad nodded. "Unfortunately, radical factions are convincing some of them to become terrorists. No one knows why they attacked us yet, but hopefully we'll have answers soon."

We didn't have answers soon. Despite what my dad and teacher had said, we were still in the dark as agonizing days went by. My friends and I went to school but couldn't concentrate on our lessons. We whispered in halls, speculated in the lunchroom, and wondered if another attack might be imminent. Sparse details emerged in sporadic waves and only blurred rather than clarified the picture. We heard about a terrorist named Osama bin Laden. We learned about the terrifying plan he had developed over many years. And we understood that our world would never be the same.

I lost my innocence on 9/11. I could no longer ride my bike, skate on an ice pond, or frolic on the beach without thinking about the 3,000 souls who could never again enjoy the things I took for granted. I could not help but frequently reflect on what had happened and what might soon happen again.

I had been shocked by the events of that day, but I was also heartened and uplifted by the response of millions in our country. Flags flew at half-mast and flapped in the breeze on every porch. Brothers and sisters of neighborhood friends enlisted in droves. On one day they had scruffy hair and blue jeans, and on the next they had buzzes or buns and wore crisp military uniforms. I watched them leave for boot camp and wondered if they'd ever come back.

Still, I was jealous. I wanted to be old enough to enlist. I felt helpless and left out. I wanted to do my part but could only observe others doing theirs. When I watched the brother of a close friend leave for boot camp, I knew that once I was old enough, I'd join the military.

My father finally opened up more and shared stories about what had happened to him while serving in Vietnam. He'd received his draft card in 1965 at twenty years old. He'd seen friends who'd joined the Army come home in body bags, so he enlisted in the Navy. Unfortunately, instead of serving his entire four years aboard a ship, they sent him to the front lines for six months. He recalled flying into Nam from the Philippines and having to run as fast as he could from the airplane while bullets whizzed past his head.

Seeing many of his friends captured or killed took a toll on my dad. I later realized that he'd been struggling with PTSD (post-traumatic stress disorder) ever since. Even so, he brought something important back from that experience: an appreciation of the simple things in life and the freedoms we enjoy. I'm very grateful that he did his best to pass this wisdom on to others, including me.

During the next several years, memories of 9/11 motivated me to become more dedicated to my martial arts training. I exercised and practiced in our basement until I was almost too exhausted to climb back up the stairs. In my tae kwon do class, I kicked and punched bags until my knuckles bled. Revenge did not motivate me so much as a sense of duty. As I watched the replays of the attack and saw the tears shed by families who'd lost loved ones that day, I was driven by a desire to ensure our country never had to endure another devastating loss like the one on 9/11.

Years later, after participating in dozens of tournaments, I finally earned a black belt. It was the summer before my senior year in high school. I was still underage, so officially it was a junior black belt, but I felt proud to have accomplished that goal without breaking a bone or my nose.

During my junior year, my music had also consumed me. I had taken advanced music theory and performed in five different orchestras. Occasionally, I had been lucky enough to play with the Cleveland Orchestra. Between practicing my roundhouse kicks and taking private music lessons, I had found little time to contemplate life or my future. When the thought had crossed my mind, I'd envisioned playing for a military orchestra. That seemed like the best of both worlds. I could serve my country while playing a viola.

Things didn't quite work out that way. In my senior year, another attack perpetrated by a Muslim extremist changed my life in ways I could never have imagined.

CHAPTER 3:

THE SECOND ATTACK

In 2005, on the fourth anniversary of 9/11, I was a senior at Ohio's largest high school. Over 3,000 students at Mentor High shared a single large two-story building. Fall covered the nearby fields with orange and gold leaves, and the building's dull red bricks and long corridors gave the school a "Cold War eighties" feel.

A brisk wind toyed with the leaves and brought the distant scent of burning wood from neighborhood fireplaces. I loved this time of year. The mornings were crisp and cool, but the days were still warm and inviting. However, on this infamous day, I could not shed the memory of the events that had unfolded four years earlier.

I recalled the fear and anger that had filled my chest as I listened to my teachers and parents describe what had happened in New York. I remembered how my heart had raced while watching the flames consume the Twin Towers. On the fourth anniversary of the devastating 9/11 attack, as news channels reminded us of the event by broadcasting images of the world's most infamous terrorist, my heart filled with sorrow and my gut filled with anger.

I did my best to quell these feelings while conversing with friends and listening to my teachers talk about chemical compounds and algebraic formulas. I also fought the urge to let my mind wander into the future and touch upon where I might be the following year after I graduated. My desire to join the military had not diminished since 9/11, but I hadn't yet decided on a branch or billet. I had been leaning toward serving in a military band so I could continue to pursue my love of music, but the recruiters I'd talked with had honestly told me that my chances of doing so were minimal.

I had mostly ruled out the Army or Marines, which left the Navy or the Air Force. My dad had served in the Navy, so that seemed like a logical choice, but the Air Force had an excellent military band, so they were still in the running. I visited with recruiters from both branches and asked dozens of questions. The Navy recruiter enticed me with the opportunity to sail to exotic shores. He made it sound like I'd be on permanent vacation on Gilligan's Island. The Air Force recruiter noticed my firm sense of right and wrong, and he suggested that I might be a perfect candidate for the Security Forces, which is essentially a military police unit. I loaded up on brochures and dreams but remained undecided.

All my friends knew I wanted to serve in the military after graduation, and some of my teachers had mentioned it during class. Only a few years removed from 9/11, many applauded and even encouraged plans to enlist. My history teacher reminded us of how patriotic the U.S. had become after the attack on Pearl Harbor—how being thrust into a war had spurred citizens to fly flags on front porches and rush down to military recruiting centers. The word "war" churned in my head, and I realized that while the world remained in constant conflict, most of us in America often turned a blind eye. Now, we could no longer stand on the sidelines.

That morning, during our lunch break, I strolled into the cafeteria with a few of my friends from orchestra class. Mike was a skinny cellist with an infectious smile and sandy blond hair. He liked to crack jokes and had assumed the role of the class clown. Sally was a shy violinist with bright red hair she pulled tight into a ponytail. She was studious, obedient, and always played by the rules. We approached the counter, filled our trays, and found some open seats. Mike made a comment that the runny mashed potatoes looked like something found in his baby brother's diaper. Sally smirked and tried to ignore him but didn't touch that part of her plate. We talked about the musical scores we were practicing and how one new song was so difficult it made us sound like a bunch of honking cars on the freeway. Eventually, the conversation wandered toward 9/11.

Sally's voice turned solemn as she recalled all the flags flying at half-mast and the images of the funeral processions. Mike tried to keep things lighter by talking about how we'd gotten payback in the 2003 Gulf War. I mentioned how I'd felt about not being able to do my part by serving in the military, but I'd finally be able to after graduation. Sally asked if I had selected a branch yet. I said I was leaning toward either the Navy or the Air Force. Mike piped in and said I should join the Army so I could drive one of those cool M1A1 Abrams tanks across the desert. I smiled and said if I had a fender bender in an Abrams, it'd take me seven lifetimes to pay off the body shop. Besides, I'd rather play in the Air Force band. Sally said she thought the Navy uniforms looked more stylish, and Mike cracked a joke about becoming Barnacle Bill the sailor.

At a table across from us, I noticed a Middle Eastern student glance at me and sneer. I hadn't met him previously, but I recalled his first name because it was Mohammed—a name I could hardly forget. I had heard that his family was Muslim, and they had immigrated from Jordan, but I knew little else about him. Some students had given Mohammed a hard time after 9/11, and I had actually felt sorry for him. I had felt sorry for other Muslims as well.

My friends and I finished our meals and dropped off our trays. A golden sun beamed through the western-facing windows and reflected off dozens of forks and knives scattered across the tables. The large cafeteria buzzed with a cacophony of youthful voices and clinking silverware. I excused myself and headed toward the men's room. Out of the corner of my eye, I noticed Mohammed get up and follow me. The hairs on my neck bristled, and I fought the urge to glance over my shoulder.

The restroom offered the fresh scent of pine as I stepped inside. Mohammed had sped up and was now a few feet behind me. Before I could approach the urinals, I felt his firm hand grip my shoulder. My heart raced as he spun me around. The boy had dark brown skin and stood almost a foot taller than me. I looked up and saw that his angry eyes burned with contempt.

Mohammed curled his lip and called me an infidel. He ridiculed me for wanting to join the military and hoped that I'd be sent to Iraq where I might get blown to bits. My knees quaked. Mohammed was much bigger and stronger, and he towered over me like Goliath over David. Even though I had a black belt, I'd only used it in competition where contact had always been light. I'd never been in an actual fight and didn't want one now. Not only did I not want to wind up in the hospital, I also didn't want to send anyone else there.

Mohammed slammed his palm into my right shoulder and started screaming at me. I didn't respond. He said I was a typical American. All talk and no action. He called me a coward for not fighting back. I wanted to but held my ground. Images from the movie *The Karate Kid* flashed into my head, and I heard Mr. Miyagi's voice whisper that martial arts were only for self-defense; I should not allow others to provoke my anger. Still, my heart pounded in my chest like a timpani in the orchestra.

Mohammed shoved me against a bathroom stall door. My head collided with the cold metal. I bit my tongue from the impact, filling my mouth with the coppery taste of blood. My hands instinctively formed fists, with rage churning inside me like the rumblings of a volcano. I fought to maintain control, struggling with where to draw the line between defending myself and allowing someone to pummel me senseless.

Mohammed's eyes narrowed as he raised his fists. He took a step closer. My heart leaped into my throat. He threw a punch at my face. My training kicked in and I dodged to the left. His fist glanced off my cheek. I pivoted right and swept my foot against his ankle. He slipped and fell sideways against a stall door. He screamed an obscenity and pulled his arm back to deliver another blow. I pictured my nose breaking and blood spurting across the tile floor. I crouched into a defensive stance and raised my arms.

The door to the men's room burst open. Mr. Green, the school's assistant principal, rushed in and ordered us to stand down. Mohammed ignored him and yelled something in a foreign language. Mr. Green raised his voice and told us again to back away from each other. I lowered my arms and stepped back. Mohammed did not. Other students poured in, pointed, and whispered as they stood behind Mr. Green. The assistant principal softened his voice and asked Mohammed to back off. Finally, he obeyed.

Mr. Green marched us both down to the principal's office. There, he demanded an explanation. I gave my side of the story while

Mohammed made it sound like I'd started it with racial slurs and comments about how "his kind" had caused 9/11. I denied the accusations, but Mr. Green didn't know who to believe, so he sentenced us both to detention. The following Saturday, I spent eight hours sitting in a room with Mohammed nearby.

At first, I was angry and upset. I hadn't started the fight; I'd only defended myself. Still, I suffered the same punishment as my assailant. I'd been forced to spend my entire Saturday sitting across from the guy who'd shoved me around and ridiculed me for joining the military. My jaw tightened as I shook my head.

The second hand on the wall clock ticked off the hours at a snail's pace. I squirmed in my seat and pretended to study something. My face flushed with anger when I occasionally glanced over at Mohammed, who looked back with hostile eyes. I closed my eyes, lowered my head, and realized that I was just as much at fault as Mohammed.

I had walked past him, and other foreign students, while hurrying to class or getting lunch in the cafeteria. I had ignored him and many others at student rallies or lounging on the grass surrounding our school. I had rarely, if ever, smiled, waved, or walked over to say hello. Although I was not a gregarious extrovert, and wasn't often outgoing, I could not use that as an excuse. I couldn't point a finger at those from different cultures for hating me if I had extended no efforts to befriend them or at least offer an olive branch.

I also recalled my discussions with several recruiters who'd said the military would offer me the chance to see the world and meet a variety of people from different lands. It occurred to me I couldn't call myself patriotic if I wasn't willing to assume the role of an American ambassador. I couldn't expect others to respect or even like

Americans if I never offered a smile or a handshake, or if I maintained an attitude of entitlement and superiority.

If I was going to represent my country as a sailor, soldier, marine, or airman, I needed to become more humble, empathetic, and approachable.

In that same moment, I also realized that regardless of how honorable my actions might be, there were still a few who would remain jaded and hateful toward the West. Some would still want to harm or kill innocent civilians, like those who had perished on 9/11. As much as I might want to change hearts and minds, I did not have control over these individuals, and I could not stand idly by while they committed acts of terrorism.

The hand on the wall clock ticked off the last second of my detention, and my chest filled with the conviction of my life's passion and purpose. I knew with certainty that I wanted to protect others from those who had become consumed by hate and malice.

A few months later, I marched down to the Air Force recruiting office and signed the papers to join the Security Forces, the military police for the Air Force.

CHAPTER 4

THE TRAINING

I graduated from high school in June 2006 and immediately moved with my family to Kingsport, Tennessee. For the rest of that month, I was on an emotional roller coaster that cycled between excited and terrified. When someone slapped me on the back to wish me luck, I smiled while shoving moist hands into my pockets.

A few weeks before my scheduled flight to Lackland Air Force Base in San Antonio, Texas, the Air Force required me to complete a thorough physical exam by a doctor at the Knoxville military entrance processing station, or MEPS. Given my ongoing tae kwon do training, I figured I was in good shape, but I was still nervous. I could fail for many reasons, including a newly discovered heart condition, an eyesight or hearing problem, or any other ailments the doctors could uncover.

Fortunately, they found nothing, so I boarded a plane on July 25, 2006. I was about to fly from Knoxville, Tennessee to San Antonio, Texas to begin my Air Force journey. As I approached the plane, I realized that my life was about to change in ways I could not even fathom. I had left behind my friends, freedoms, and family. I was about to embark on a journey where I'd hopefully gain new friends and defend the freedoms I'd been privileged to enjoy, but I knew I'd miss my family. Upon arrival, I sat on a cold Air Force bus seat and listened to dozens of crickets chirp in the midnight air, I watched a handful of other recruits climb aboard. Their eyes, I was sure, resembled mine—full of trepidation, wonder, and hope.

The military loves acronyms. They have one for everything. Boot camp for the Air Force is called basic military training, or BMT. It's a six-week program of rigorous physical and combat training that is not for the faint of heart. My heart was not faint, but it still fluttered as the bus pulled up to the front gate of the base. The dull gray buildings reminded me of a prison, and I felt like an inmate on my way to an execution.

BMT begins with the Zero Week receiving phase that is anything but welcoming. Only a half-dozen of us had boarded the bus that first night, but we were told that almost fifty more recruits were arriving within a day. We all reeked of sweat and fear as a military training instructor, or MTI, escorted us into our barracks. He wore a crisp, blue uniform and a wide-brimmed Smokey the Bear hat—or cover—that made him look like a forest ranger.

While we were still in civilian clothes, and sporting non-regulation haircuts, an MTI assigned us to a squadron and a flight. The instructors searched us for contraband during a shakedown and then rushed us up to our dorm rooms where they assigned us an uncomfortable bed and a small wall locker. They designated this as our personal living area (PLA). My head started pounding as I tried to remember all the abbreviations.

Nervous and disoriented, I didn't sleep for more than a few hours in my rack that first night. The next morning, MTIs shocked us awake with the sound of kicked trash cans and abundant screaming. One banged a stick on a trash can lid while ordering us to get out of our racks and stand at attention. With my heart pounding and my eyes blurry, I stood on the cold tile floor and shivered, certain that I was about to experience the worst day of my life.

Queasy anticipation had prevented me from eating much the prior week, but that morning, I was starving. They told us we'd get three meals a day during "chow time" at the DFAC, the dining facility "chow hall." While on field training exercises, we'd dine on the ever-so-tasty meals ready-to-eat (MRE) packs that were about as appealing as a microwave dinner.

They marched us over to the chow hall where the scent of bacon made my mouth water. Then the agony began. While being yelled at to keep a tight formation, with our stomachs growling, we stood in a long line for twenty-five minutes. Finally, they slapped a sampling of food on our trays and told us we had only five minutes to scarf it down. I tasted almost nothing as I shoveled scrambled eggs past my teeth. While my weight was fine, I noticed that some recruits appeared either under or overweight and recalled my recruiter saying that in such cases, meals were doubled or halved, respectively. I smiled at the thought, as an underweight, "skinny" recruit might never have enough time to eat a double ration.

We carried our trays to the kitchen area, where "chow runners" shoved them onto an assembly line to be cleaned by the kitchen staff. Aside from the clanking and clacking of utensils and plates, the chow hall was mostly silent as no one had time to chat and few of us had anything to say anyway.

While we squelched burps from eating too fast, our MTIs granted us five minutes to phone home. I let my mom and dad know I had arrived safely, and the instructors had not killed or maimed me. At least not yet. My eyes misted as I heard my mom's worried voice, and for a fleeting moment, I wondered if I'd made a huge mistake.

Our next stop was the base barber shop where a burly man flashed an ominous grin before turning on his electric razor and trimming my head bald. During my buzz cut, I watched brown chunks of my hair fall to the tiled floor while suffering another pang of remorse. I again wondered if I'd made a bad decision.

With my head resembling a bowling ball and my eyelids heavy from lack of sleep, I tried to keep from swaying in the breeze while standing on a grassy field near the barracks. The MTI assigned to our "Baby Flight" was a tall master sergeant with a trim mustache, square jaw, and broad shoulders. He had a deep, commanding voice and delivered a synopsis of the training we were about to receive. Our MTI said that during the next two months, we'd be cordially compelled to complete Air Force crash courses on military discipline, physical fitness, ceremonies, drills, weaponry, and basic fighting skills. He then pointed toward one building where we'd begin our adventure.

In our first day of class, I learned that after World War II, on February 4, 1946, they moved Air Force BMT to Lackland from the air base at Harlingen, Texas. Since then, over seven million recruits had attended, but not all had graduated. I also learned that several months earlier, on November 7, 2005, the BMT curriculum had been altered to focus on a "warrior first" type of airman. I wondered if the millions of airmen who'd completed the prior training across sixty years had been taught to be "warriors second," but I kept my thoughts private.

The next few days included more yelling and banging followed by marching, lectures, and five-minute meals. They did not issue us uniforms until that Friday, and in the meantime, they called us "rainbows" while pointing at our varied and bright civilian clothing. When they finally issued our uniforms, base personnel slapped clothing articles into our outstretched arms.

We ended our orientation week at Lackland by filling out a mound of forms, getting jabbed with a dozen vaccination needles, and completing a rigorous physical fitness test that left us all breathless. The test consisted of one-minute pushups and sit-ups followed by a brisk 1.5-mile run. During the run, a recruit started wheezing until his eyes rolled up. He fell to the ground in a heap. They rushed him to the "Medical Hold" flight—an obvious oxymoron—where they discovered he had asthma that had been missed in his pre-BMT medical exam. We were now down to fifty-four recruits, but I knew the attrition had only just begun. While I had often wondered if my enlistment decision had been ill-advised, I now prayed that I'd make it through the next several weeks.

During the next week, when we screwed up, which seemed often and inevitable, our disciplinary action came as added workouts. More pushups, squat thrusts, flutter kicks, or an extra mile. Those who refused to comply with Air Force rules or could not keep up were drummed out or set back by a week or two. The last thing any of us wanted was to remain in BMT for an extra day, let alone another seven or fourteen days. We were told that to graduate, we had to achieve minimum scores in frequent physical and written tests. Those who barely passed received "Liberator" designations, while they labeled those who excelled as "Thunderbolt" or "Warhawk."

In the third week of my boot camp experience, they handed me an M16 rifle. I knew which end was which, of course, but during this week of training, I learned how to disassemble, assemble, clean, repair, and properly stow my rifle. On an outdoor range, they showed me how to load, aim, and properly fire my weapon. At first, I couldn't hit the side of a semi-truck from point blank range. With some practice, and again leveraging my martial arts training, I controlled my breathing and relaxed enough to hit the outer target rings. Eventually, I centered more often on the bullseye.

Week four was intense, but also invigorating. I smacked my fellow recruits around in rifle-fighting class, crawled on my belly through the sand course, learned how to flash silent hand signals, and concluded the week with CBRNE training. This impossible-to-pronounce acronym stands for chemical, biological, radiological, nuclear, and explosives. No one I know can say that five times quickly without getting tongue twisted. This training taught me that few can survive any of these attacks. Certainly not if they're perpetrated effectively. All one can do is hope the enemy is a bad shot or you can last long enough to counterattack. In one exercise, our MTI handed us gas masks and then grinned. He herded us into a small bunker and slammed the door shut. The dark room filled with white gas. The MTIs then ordered us to remove our masks.

I felt nothing at first. Thirty seconds later, my eyes watered and my lungs burned. I coughed, cried, and prayed that someone would open the door. Trapped and in pain, I felt the fingers of panic grip my throat. Long, agonizing minutes passed before the bunker door flew open. We rushed outside, bent over, and coughed or vomited for another twenty minutes while the instructors pointed and laughed. After our ordeal, however, they treated us differently, as if we'd completed some sort of ritual that transitioned us to "Almost Airmen." Even so, we would not—*could not*—become full-fledged airmen until we had completed Warrior Week.

To complete Warrior Week, we had to pass one of our toughest tests. This is where the MTIs gave us the opportunity to apply everything we'd learned so far while completing realistic field exercises and combat scenarios. If we failed, they'd set us back by a week or two—a recruit's worst nightmare.

The five-day ordeal began with combative wrestling. Most of us gained a few black and blue bruises during these, and I was fortunate to pass without looking like someone had mugged me in a dark alley. Next, they weighted us down with heavy body armor, equipment, two canteens, and sent us out to a site with four zones. These were simulated forward operating bases, and each one contained a ring of ten field tents centered around a three-story observation tower. A hardened briefing facility served as a bomb shelter and armory. I wondered why anyone would want to store bombs inside a bomb shelter but decided not to voice my opinion. Each zone was defended by five defensive firing positions stacked with sandbags. Our job required keeping bad guys out of our zone and repelling any attacks.

During this exciting week of war games, the MTIs invited us to shred various targets with high-powered M16A2 rifles. The targets were man-sized and placed at twenty-one meters distance. They gave us twenty-four rounds and we had to take aim while standing, kneeling, sitting, or lying prone. We had to hit the targets at least seventeen out of twenty-four times to pass, and if we landed twenty-two rounds, we qualified for the Small Arms Expert Marksmanship Ribbon. I enjoyed this part of our training and was fortunate to land twenty-three shots on target.

Now that we could handle small arms without shooting ourselves in the foot, we learned how to conduct unexploded ordnance (UXO) sweeps. We all paid close attention during this training as improvised explosive devices, or IEDs, were commonplace in locales like Iraq or Afghanistan. In one exercise, we patrolled a 1.5-mile-long trail littered with IEDs. Even though the bombs were not live, all of us dripped with sweat and fought to keep our hands steady while making our way down a roadside lane in tactical formation. We squinted and scanned each side of the road for signs of an IED buried under debris, soda cans, or foliage. The MTIs did not task us with disarming or removing these, but instead showed us how to find, avoid, and report them.

At the end of the trail, we broke out into teams of two wingmen to negotiate a combat obstacle course. This often required turning our bodies into twisted pretzels to low crawl, hide behind walls, roll behind barriers, wiggle through mud, or whack dummies with the butt of our rifle. We also did sixty-yard-high crawls up a forty-five-degree angle through a pit of deep sand. It took me a week to get all that dirt off my body.

During Warrior Week, our class took part in a CLAW mission, which stands for creating leader airmen warriors. For this exercise, they gave us minimal supplies and instructions before we traversed a simulated river, where teamwork became crucial to our "survival." We then moved in staggered tactical formation to another checkpoint before facing our most difficult combat obstacle course.

Should the unthinkable happen while on an actual mission, we received hands-on training in CPR, first aid, and buddy care. We learned how to properly rescue a downed airman while under fire from snipers and gunners in the village. Some of us "didn't make it," and the instructors evaluated us on how many were still "alive" at the end of the exercise. All of us who passed the training proudly clipped on our dog tags, printed with our names, numbers, and blood types.

The sixth week of BMT focused mostly on post-deployment training. During this week, the MTIs gave us intensive classroom instruction on the difficulties some of us might face after returning from a tough deployment. Examples included PTSD, financial struggles, family or relationship issues, and alcohol or substance abuse. I didn't think I'd ever have to worry about any of those, but paid attention anyway.

Lest we forgot our previous training, we participated in multiple drills and dorm inspections while learning about Air Force history and heritage. This less stressful week ended with a final physical fitness test. Those who failed, with their heads hung low, were set back by a week to the "Get Fit" flight where the workouts were intense and ongoing.

Getting through week six also required a passing grade on the Air Force End of Course written exam, which we completed on Friday. The MTIs required us to attain a score of seventy or greater to avoid a setback, and if we achieved ninety or better, it resulted in an honor grad candidacy.

Once I'd completed the exam, they granted me the privilege of participating in the Airman's Run—a two-mile formation run that celebrates the esprit de corps gained during airmen training. Breathless and smiling, those still with us attended the Coin and Retreat Ceremony where they presented us with the Airman's Challenge Coin, signifying our transition from trainees to full-fledged airmen. No longer Baby Flights, we were officially part of the U.S. Air Force.

Graduating on time from boot camp will always be one of the proudest and memorable accomplishments of my life. None of us were heroes. We hadn't survived a war or tragedy; had not solved world hunger or cured cancer; but together, as a team, we had helped each other transition from boys to men. We had gained the discipline, skills, and trust needed to rely on each other, perhaps for our mutual survival. Most of all, we had learned that we are not alone in this world. We learned how to have respect and compassion for those on our left and right.

That Friday, my hands were steady and my gaze unwavering as I stood in front of the barracks mirror and buttoned up my uniform. In a tight formation, with a brass band playing military cadences, we marched in front of bleachers full of family and friends during the graduation parade. With my heart pounding, I could hardly refrain from beaming broadly while keeping my eyes forward. After the parade, my parents found me in the formation of Airmen. My mom wrapped her arms around me and didn't let go for a full minute. My dad had to pry her away so he could shake my hand. His eyes misted with pride, and so did mine.

I gave them a tour of the base, including the dorm and authorized areas. As we passed by one of the training fields, I noticed a few airmen I had befriended during BMT. They were panting and sweating while doing dozens of flutter kicks. My heart sank. They had almost made it all the way but had failed the final physical exam, so they had been held back a week. While I was glad I had finally graduated, I regretted that a few in our class had not. At least not yet.

The MTIs gave me a town pass so I could venture through the streets of San Antonio with my family. The first thing I wanted was a half-pound cheeseburger and a mound of greasy fries, followed by a slice of homemade apple pie—with ice cream. We visited the famous Alamo on the outskirts of town, and my chest tightened as I thought about the brave souls who had made the ultimate sacrifice to defend what appeared to be a worthless and rundown structure. Having completed BMT, which had included several realistic combat scenarios, I realized that the soldiers who had died at the Alamo had not fought to defend a mound of mud and stucco. They had died defending each other. They had given their all for the guy on the left and right.

The following Monday morning, a surge of excitement rushed through my veins when they handed me an envelope containing my orders. Even though my fourteen weeks of Security Forces training would all be at Lackland, on the other side of the base from BMT, I had only been provided with sparse details related to the type of instruction I'd receive. As a bright sun warmed the desert sand surrounding San Antonio, I gazed at a mirage on a distant horizon and wondered what lay ahead in the next chapter of my life.

CHAPTER 5:

DEAD AGAIN

The next chapter of my life started with sweaty palms and a short bus ride from one side of the San Antonio base to the other. The bus screeched to a halt, and the Security Forces Tech School instructors rushed us into a barracks that looked exactly like the one we'd just left. I felt like I'd gone back in time to my first day of boot camp. Minutes after stowing our gear, they carted us off to our first day of class. This consisted of an orientation designed to help us become aware of and deal with potential mental, academic, and social obstacles we might face in the next phase of our training.

During the next week, we spent a lot of time squirming in classroom seats before our instructors allowed us to step out into the hot Texas sun and play with guns. We'd done this in boot camp, of course, but now our training became more intense. We received more advanced instruction on the M4 carbine assault rifle, which is essentially an AR-15, as well as the M9 Beretta 9mm pistol and the M249 5.56mm and M240 Bravo 7.62mm machine guns. Those bad boys are loud. We also learned how to toss exploding hand grenades, including fragmentation grenades. All of us dripped with nervous sweat as we threw a few live ones into sand pits and then crouched behind metal barriers to avoid getting hit with shrapnel.

We learned a few next-level hand-to-hand combat techniques, including how to take down suspects without breaking their bones… or ours. Our instructors taught us where to deliver tactical blows to debilitate difficult perpetrators, which entailed using a few jiu-jitsu techniques. Given my martial arts experience, I loved this part of our training. We were told not to exert full power during any of these moves to keep from hurting ourselves or others. Fortunately, none of us got pretzel-twisted to the point of fracturing a limb, but we'd heard horror stories about other classes where a "macho dude" had gone too far and sent a fellow trainee to the medical unit.

Once we'd completed a few weeks of classroom and preparatory instruction, our instructors gave us MOUT training. Yet another acronym that stands for military operations in urban terrain. They handed us AR-15s and M9s and loaded us into Air Force patrol cars. While driving around, our radio crackled, and a dispatcher told us to investigate an active shooter in a building. In one scenario, as the designated driver, I gunned the engine and did a fast U-turn toward a compromised building. I careened around a corner and slammed on the brakes.

We then grabbed our weapons and gear and popped open the vehicle doors. A hot desert wind fanned my face as I crouched behind the driver's door and glanced up at the five-story building. I scanned each window but saw nothing. I looked over at my three colleagues. They flashed signals indicating they also saw no flashes or faces. I signaled back that we should sprint toward the entrance. The four of us ran in unison across the asphalt. Ten feet from the door, all hell broke loose.

One instructor, acting as a terrorist on an upper floor, started shooting at us. Although he fired blanks, the pops were loud and realistic. Adrenaline accelerated my legs, and I darted inside and bent over to catch my breath. The four of us then went from room to room while yelling "clear" after checking the hard corners.

Even though the shooting had come from an upper floor, our instructors had taught us to check each room along the way. That's what we were supposed to do, but on our first few runs, we messed up and missed a room or two. In almost every case, an instructor popped out from inside and shot one of us in the face. When it happened to me, even though I knew the guy had fired blanks, I nearly peed my pants. For a split second, I really felt like I'd just been killed.

Sometimes, even though we'd checked a room, we occasionally got tunnel vision and missed a hard corner or failed to see an instructor hiding in the shadows. When we turned to leave, we heard several loud pops as the role-playing terrorist shot us in the back. Sometimes we'd assume someone was an innocent bystander in a situation until they pulled a gun from a pocket and blew us away.

In one scenario, an instructor came running over to me and acted like a civilian in distress. He pointed toward a building and said there were terrorists inside with machine guns. Of course, I believed him and signaled for our team to investigate. I had failed to notice that the guy wore a long, black trench coat in the middle of a scorching desert. He opened the coat and exposed a vest loaded with explosives. He then grinned and pulled a cord. Dead again. After weeks of dying, I felt like a character in a video game that can't get past level one.

Over time, we built up muscle memory and improved. Our vision became more attuned to various situations. We detected details we had missed before, reacted faster, and stopped dying as often. I was grateful for this as I knew that in the real world, faced with similar situations, the ordeals would be ten times more intense—and ten times more lethal.

As the weeks went by, I also formed a bond with my teammates, and they with me. We learned how to trust each other and knew that we had each other's backs. There were a few individuals who were a bit arrogant, had a cocky attitude, or thought they were bullet-proof bad asses. None of them survived long. They died along with the rest of us, and most of them finally swallowed their pride. A few never did and were invited to leave. Others couldn't handle the book learning and tough tests, the physical demands, or the intense and constant stress. We started with a class of almost 130 security force trainees, but only 85 of us graduated.

Along the way, we learned how to rely on each other to secure airfields, base buildings, and handle terrorist threats and drunk drivers. We completed combat patrols in simulated war zones—such as Iraq or Afghanistan. In one scenario, our instructors taught us how to initiate meetings with local tribe leaders to obtain intel on the bad guys. We learned how to recognize improvised explosive devices on the side of a road and keep an airman alive when wounded. If a bomb disabled our Humvee, we'd have to finish our mission on foot through IED mine fields and past dilapidated buildings filled with gun-wielding terrorist "tangos." We were told that our job could entail taking down Taliban operatives, serving on a presidential detail, protecting a missile silo loaded with unconventional weapons, or a variety of other missions. Our responsibilities were diverse, dangerous, and difficult.

Sometimes the training was so difficult I didn't think I was going to make it. I thought I'd be one of the dozens that either quit or got drummed out. That's when I'd feel the hand of a fellow airman help me up a hill, catch me when I fell, or give me a pat on the back to keep me going. While watching my colleagues perform in realistic situations, my chest filled with pride. I felt honored to be serving alongside these dedicated men and women who were sacrificing so much to protect others. There were a few who only saw their military careers as stepping-stones to something more, but most genuinely wanted to make a difference. They wanted to keep our country safe and prevent another 9/11.

On December 21, 2006, when I finally completed the fifteenth week of training, I was both relieved and elated. I received my official Air Force Security Forces badge and beret. While wearing both in the middle of the graduation hall, I gazed at the memorial wall that listed the names and ranks of the Security Forces airmen who'd fallen in the line of duty. I reflected on this for a long moment and realized that they had all completed this training and walked through this same hall before being sent to their various commands.

Less than a week later, the Air Force invited me to report to Lajes Field in the Azores. I had no idea where that was and had to look it up on a map. I flew home to spend the Christmas holidays with my family, and in the second week of January 2007, I boarded a plane bound for Portugal.

CHAPTER 6:

THE ACCIDENT

I departed the United States on a commercial flight bound for Lisbon, the capital of Portugal. Upon arrival, since my flight to Lajes Field wasn't until the next morning, I explored Lisbon for several hours before returning to my hotel. Excited about my first assignment, I tossed and turned on the hard mattress most of the night.

The Azores is a collection of nine small islands that sit off the coast of Portugal. The country is known for its welcoming and friendly population, breathtaking landscapes, sleepy fishing villages, and expansive green pastures. Volcanic mountain peaks and bubbling hot springs surround the ancient fishing ports, which are mostly quiet save for the occasional roar of jet aircraft in the distance. Our plane descended toward Lajes Field on Terceira Island and lumbered to a halt. We stretched, grabbed our luggage, and disembarked.

I expected a hot and humid climate, perhaps something akin to Hawaii, but it was cold and damp that day in mid-January 2007. I closed my eyes and breathed in the sweet scent of blue hydrangeas delivered from an array of endless hedgerows near the airfield. The 65th Air Base Group operates Lajes and shares the airfield with the civilian airport, which services the entire Island of Terceira. That time of year, with wintry winds buffeting the tarmac and few tourists arriving, the airport felt like a ghost town.

While preparing for my deployment, I read that back in 1928, a Portuguese Army lieutenant colonel wrote a formal report suggesting the construction of Lajes Field. The Portuguese *Aeronáutica Militar* (Army Aviation) overruled him and instead chose the island of São Miguel. They reversed that decision a few years later after condemning the São Miguel airfield due to rough weather and inadequate dimensions.

During World War II, the Portuguese built and expanded the Lajes runway and rumbled in a squadron of Gloster Gladiator fighters. Portuguese Junkers Ju 52 started flying cargo missions in July 1942. The Americans and Brits flocked in toward the end of the war and hammered together even more expansions while sending flights of anti-submarine warfare (ASW) aircraft to hunt down German U-boats in the Atlantic. This helped turn the tide of the war by allowing more transport ships to resupply Allied troops in France and Germany. By the end of the war, given that the airfield reduced transatlantic flight time by almost half, several thousand American planes had used the field. This set the stage for an eventual U.S. Air Force occupation in the fifties.

A member of my unit picked me up at the airport and drove me to the dormitory on the military side of the airfield. Although in good repair, the aging brick and mortar building made me feel like I had been transported back in time. The Bing Crosby song, "Don't Fence Me In," played in my head as I stepped from the vehicle and ambled inside.

During our first week, the base personnel gave us an orientation and helped us get settled in. There were fewer than 2,000 Americans on the island and only about sixty-five people in my unit. At first, I didn't know anyone save for a few guys I'd traveled with. I'm not overtly outgoing, so it took me several weeks to form a few friendships. I was four hours ahead of my family in the States and finding time to call home was difficult.

During my training, I learned that the Lajes Air Base was predominately an Air Force gas station in the Atlantic. While the airfield was strategically important, we weren't in a war zone and did not expect any terrorist attacks. Still, we enforced the law as security personnel and kept the base safe. We were essentially military patrolmen who responded to domestic violence calls, drunk driving incidents, building alarms, or aircraft security alerts on the flight line.

I completed two weeks of orientation before they assigned me to a flight where I completed another sixty days of on-the-job training. During that time, I did frequent ride-alongs in Air Force police cars with experienced security personnel. I also completed various tasks, without mistakes, before assuming full-fledged patrol duties. On every patrol, they required us to have Portuguese Air Force security personnel with us. While Americans occupied most of the base, there were some Portuguese nationals and military personnel. The Air Force forbade us to do anything more than observe incidents involving these individuals. Ultimately, the Portuguese security partner had the final say in all matters, even for situations involving Americans.

During my first few months, I relied heavily on my supervisor, David Stone, an E-5 staff sergeant who helped me understand and follow all the rules. He was a stocky guy with brown hair and hazel eyes, and he often flashed a friendly smile. He was also an excellent leader who taught me a valuable lesson that I live by to this day:

always take care of your people. He genuinely cared about everyone on his team and always went to bat for us when needed.

He reported to Edward Barber, an approachable and personable E-6 technical sergeant. Edward was an outgoing Hispanic man whose family had immigrated from Colombia. He displayed a great deal of wisdom and patience, and also took care of his team. He often invited us over to his home where his wife made a fantastic meal while we played endless games of Texas Hold'em. I wasn't much of a poker player and rarely won, but I always looked forward to the experience. Both he and David became my mentors during my time in the Azores, and their guidance affected my career and life. Over time, they helped mold me into a better security airman and a better person.

During my third month on the island, Edward tapped me on the shoulder and invited me to participate in an Air Force fundraising tradition called Jail and Bail. This was the only time junior-ranking personnel could pull one over on high-ranking officers. The base invited Americans on the island to pay money—as donations for worthwhile charities—to have an Air Force member arrested and thrown into a fake jail. Security Forces Airmen would then carry out the arrest warrant.

Edward called for a young lieutenant to be arrested and asked me to apprehend the "perp." Being new to the game, I didn't remember all the rules—such as no unsafe chasing or physical contact, including grabbing or tackling. When I arrived at the lieutenant's work center, he sprinted in the opposite direction. I tried to grab him, which I wasn't supposed to do, and pulled off one of his shoes. Laughing and scrambling, the officer ran down a flight of stairs—which he wasn't supposed to do. Edward saw that everyone had broken the rules, and that I was losing the game, so he charged after the lieutenant, which he wasn't supposed to do. The officer dodged left just as Edward leapt right. Edward slammed his head hard against a beam. Dazed and bleeding, he fell to the floor. I bolted down the stairs and helped him back to his feet. He was smacked up and hobbling, but otherwise seemed fine. When the lieutenant stopped running and came back to check on his tech sergeant, I whipped out my handcuffs and arrested him. He frowned and then smiled while awkwardly handing Edward a handkerchief.

Edward taught me a valuable lesson that day. Although he almost always followed the rules, his team came first. When he saw I was struggling because the officer had broken the rules, he did the right thing, which was to back up his guys. He could have gotten into trouble but that didn't matter. I later completed a few leadership training courses and have read some books on the topic, but they all pale in comparison to Edward's example of true servant leadership.

Eventually, after arresting a few officers and throwing them into a fake jail, I ventured off base with some of my new friends to explore the surrounding area. One of those friends, also new to the base, was Amber Anderson. She was a petite, E-4 senior airman, one rank senior to me, with short brown hair and hazel eyes. Amber was a playful soul, and while she was attractive, we didn't have any romantic chemistry. Instead, she became a close friend—more like a sister—and we explored the island together.

We discovered that yachts making the transatlantic passage between the United States and Europe often make pit stops in the Azores. An airman told us that the marina in Horta, on the island of Faial, had a jetty with an open-air gallery covered in murals painted by some crews that frequent the port. He described Peter's Cafe Sport, a famous yachtsmen's bar, where you can grab a beer and mingle with crews from around the world. You can also charter a boat and sail around the islands while watching schools of dolphins play in the aquamarine waters.

Others on the base described various volcanic landscapes and spa retreats that offered dips in the island's natural geothermal hot springs along with oil massages. I wasn't sure I could afford the latter but looked forward to enjoying the former. In my first few months on the island, I treated myself to some of the best food in the world. The Quinta dos Açores is a dairy farm on the island that serves its own locally produced beef and a brand of homemade ice cream mingled with fresh coconut and pineapple.

Given our busy schedule, we rarely got the chance to venture far, so our favorite hangout became a strip of bars in a nearby town called Praia that offered Sagres—a tasty and inexpensive Portuguese beer. Along the same street, we could also get a slice of pizza or enjoy a nice meal at a small restaurant, and then take a short stroll over to a gorgeous beach with white sand and lapping waves. There were times when I felt like I was in paradise.

While sipping on bottles of Sagres, we listened to fado music that combined melancholic chord progressions with interesting musical patterns I'd never heard before. Given my orchestra background, I found myself captivated by these tunes, which were usually performed in pubs by local guitarists and singers, and seemed to reflect the dramatic and moody weather of the Azores. On my days off, I occasionally drove up to the top of a mountain peak where I could be alone for a time and thank God for giving me the opportunity to be stationed one street away from heaven.

I didn't swim much in my first few months on the island as the water temperature hovered in the low sixties, but I was told that the diving during the summer, when the ocean warmed to the mid-seventies, was spectacular. This was especially true around the pinnacles at Princess Alice Bank where you could see schools of mobulas, large manta rays, and migrating humpback whales. I'd never been much of a diver, but decided I'd give it a try when the weather turned. In the meantime, I spent most of my days diving into my new job.

On one occasion, the Air Force One jet, ferrying George W. Bush, made a brief stopover at Lajes. None of us got to see the president, but we gawked and pointed at the jet as it sat on the runway and refueled. After that, three months passed with only a few minor incidents involving angry couples throwing pots and pans at each other or a drunk airman who needed corralling and a ride back to the base.

When a summer sun finally started fanning the island with golden rays that reflected off the clear blue waters, I was feeling more at home at Lajes. By now, I was fully trained, had several new friends, and no longer felt like a high school newbie. On a bright Saturday morning, they handed me the keys to a police car and told me to patrol an area off the base. Along with my Portuguese security ride-along, I spent several hours in the morning cruising past various facilities, storage areas, and local homes. At the end of my shift, while looking forward to a mug of Sagres beer and a platter of local cuisine, I steered back toward the base. Cattle roamed free on the island, and a small herd, taking their time to cross a road, delayed us for about twenty minutes. Once the cattle passed, I rounded a corner near the base and spied a local taxi—painted black and yellow—speeding down the street. My eyes widened when I realized the driver was headed toward a stop sign while speeding at fifty miles per hour.

Suddenly, tires screeched to a halt and a plume of smoke billowed from the back of the taxi. I heard a clank followed by a loud thud and the sound of breaking glass. I strained to see what had happened, but we were too far away. I gunned the engine, pulled up close, and scrambled out of the police car. My Portuguese partner stayed in the car to radio in the incident.

As I approached, the driver of the taxi opened his door. He looked first at his smashed windshield and then gaped at a spot near the front of his vehicle. I followed his eyes. On the ground near the bumper lay a mangled bicycle. A wrinkled tire spun in endless circles. Nearby, a young boy with black hair, no older than fifteen, lay motionless on the ground. Blood pooled around his head and foam bubbles gurgled from his mouth.

Instinct and training kicked in. Recalling Warrior Week in boot camp, where I'd been trained to rescue downed airmen, I rushed over and knelt by the boy. I could tell he'd likely broken his right arm and the back of his head had been split open. A pool of crimson had formed on the black asphalt. Being careful not to move his neck in case he had suffered a spinal injury, I pulled off my uniform's shirt and used it to wrap the boy's head to stop the bleeding.

Once the boy was stable, I ran back to my car and grabbed a tire iron while my partner placed traffic cones around the scene. I sprinted back to the bicycle, ripped off my belt, and made a splint for the boy's arm. The taxi driver, a Portuguese national, sat in the driver's seat in shock while muttering something unintelligible. I tried to calm him down and asked if he spoke English. He did, but barely, so my Portuguese partner translated. The taxi driver insisted that the bicycle had come flying out of nowhere and slammed into his car. I knew otherwise. I had witnessed the accident and knew he'd been speeding and had raced past the stop sign. I didn't argue with him, as I figured the local authorities would sort things out later.

I knelt again by the boy, checked his vitals, and said a silent prayer. A few minutes later, the blare of sirens filled the air. An ambulance raced over, followed by a local police car. EMTs wheeled in a gurney, and using great care, placed the boy into the ambulance. One medic, using broken English, thanked me for saving the kid's life. I wasn't sure I had, but I was grateful that the young lad was still alive.

Later that day, Edward and David both praised me for acting quickly and taking the appropriate action. At the time, I didn't think much of it, as I was just doing my job. I figured anyone else on the team would have done the same thing. A month later, Edward called me into his office. My throat tightened as I thought I'd done something wrong and was about to be dressed down. Edward stood as I walked in. A cavern formed between his eyes. My knees buckled, and I was grateful when he asked me to take a seat. He also sat and grabbed a folder from his desk. He opened it and pulled out a sheet of paper. My shirt fluttered with every heartbeat as my mind explored everything I might have done wrong over the past month. Had I accidentally broken a rule or messed up an assignment?

Edward cleared his throat and read from the document. My ears burned and then abruptly cooled. I wasn't being disciplined. I was getting a medal—an Air Force Commendation Medal. For a lowly airman, this was a rare occasion. Edward explained that he and David had originally recommended me for the Air Force Achievement Medal, but it had been upgraded due to my actions during the recent bicycle accident. The medics had determined that had I not acted so quickly and correctly, the boy might not have lived. At the very least, his injuries might have been more debilitating and long lasting. I still didn't think I deserved a medal but was glad that I'd been able to help the young boy, who I'd been told had recovered completely.

Fall in the Azores is nothing like Mentor, Ohio. No maple leaves coat the ground in burnt orange, no frosty mist tickles your nose in the early morning, and no one is suiting up to play a football game. Still, I definitely felt a change of season as summer ended during my first year on the island. Even though I still wasn't sure why I'd earned a medal, I was far more comfortable with my new environment and job and had made several new friends during my first nine months. I felt proficient and capable in my role as a military cop and had no reason to suspect that I'd make any rookie mistakes that could ruin my career.

One Friday evening, during a late shift, the radio lit up with a routine call to swing by the enlisted person's club and assist an intoxicated airman. Edward had previously explained that these courtesy rides were another way we could take care of our people so they didn't get a driving under the influence (DUI) citation, or worse, get into an accident and hurt themselves or others.

The call came in near the end of my shift. I glanced at my watch and then at my Portuguese security partner in the passenger seat. He was a short, muscular guy with dark hair and a trimmed mustache. His name was Alfredo Santos, but he preferred Al. I explained the situation to Al and said we probably did not have enough time to swing by, dump the drunk guy into the backseat, whisk him to his residence, and get back in time before our shift ended. He frowned and said he'd like to stay longer and help, but he had plans with his family that evening and could not be late.

I nodded and said I understood. I didn't think it would be a problem if I did this one solo. I figured it was just a routine ride home with little chance of anything going awry.

I was wrong.

CHAPTER 7:

DUI

On a warm night in the Azores, now on my own, I pulled up to the nightclub and stepped out of the vehicle. I sauntered inside and nodded at a guy named Joe, a big burly bouncer who often guarded the door to the club. He nodded toward a bar stool. I walked over and tapped a tipsy airman on the shoulder and asked if he was ready for a ride home. He flashed me a puzzled look and pointed to his left. I turned my head.

A young woman, with her blond hair fanning the bar, was out cold. Drool ran from one side of her mouth and mingled with rivers of beer on the wooden bar. Gingerly, I reached over and rested my palm on her back. I shook a few times to wake her up. No response. I shook a few more times. Still nothing. Finally, I smacked her back until she finally lifted her head.

She uttered a stream of slurred profanities and then placed her head back onto the bar. I shook her awake again and said it was time to leave. She flung my arm away, and using a few choice words, told me to leave her alone. I said I was with security and needed to give her a ride home. She didn't care and again told me to fornicate myself.

I nodded at Joe, and together we wrested her away from the bar and dragged her out to my police car. On the way, I glimpsed her face. I had seen her a few times previously, either at local bars or in the base cafeteria. I didn't recall her name but thought it might be Cathy or Karen. I remembered she was an E-6 tech sergeant and so outranked me by three levels.

As I shut the door to the police car, warning bells went off in my head. I probably should not be alone with a female enlisted person, especially an intoxicated one, while driving her home. In her current state, something could be misconstrued later—something completely above board perceived as something that was not.

I glanced at Cathy, if that was her name, then at my radio, and then back at the half-asleep woman in the back seat. I looked at my watch and thought about that bottle of beer waiting for me. I shrugged and decided that given Cathy's current state, this would be a simple ride home and there was nothing to worry about.

I shook Cathy awake enough to have her slur out an address. Twenty minutes later, I pulled up in front of her apartment, opened the car door, and helped the inebriated woman to her feet. She stumbled her way down the sidewalk and into her home. Finally relieved of the burden of drunk Cathy, I was glad that the event was over, and I could put this night behind me.

No such luck.

I called in to report that I'd successfully escorted the female tech sergeant from the bar to her home, and I was ending my shift. After a moment of silence, the dispatcher said they needed me to stay on duty awhile longer. Another security airman had been detained at an incident, and there had been reports of a disturbance in my area.

They wanted me to wait for a Portuguese security partner to arrive and then patrol the neighborhood with him. I figured the reported disturbance was probably laughing Cathy but thought it best not to mention this. Frustrated at having my shift extended, I acknowledged the order and sat in my car until the Portuguese security partner showed up. Turns out, we knew each other. His name was Fernando Alvarez, and he sported a broad smile and bushy beard. We started walking the streets. By now, I had picked up enough Portuguese to converse lightly, and he knew just enough English to convey a few thoughts. I did my best to explain what had happened with Cathy. About an hour later, we finally wrapped up our foot patrol and walked back to our vehicles. I smiled, certain that my workday was finally over.

I waved at Fernando, reached for my police car door handle, and then froze. Out of the corner of my eye, I caught a glimpse of Cathy driving by in a Toyota Corolla. I was shocked. Less than two hours earlier, I had directed the inebriated woman toward her home. The car disappeared around a corner before Fernando had also seen Cathy driving. We hurried back to my patrol car and made our way to Cathy's apartment. I exited my vehicle, approached Cathy's Toyota, and placed my palm on the hood. It was warm. I shook my head. She had obviously taken a spin while intoxicated. I struggled with what to do next. If we arrested her, we could ruin her career.

Standing in the cool night air, while trying to decide what to do, Edward's voice filled my head. I heard him say that I should always take care of my people. At first, I interpreted that as letting Cathy off the hook but then quickly realized I needed to do just the opposite. By driving drunk, Cathy could have hurt or killed someone—perhaps one of "our people." In this case, taking care of our people meant keeping them safe. I recalled how the taxi driver had sped through a stop sign and almost killed the boy on the bike. I could not allow that to happen. If I let this incident go, Cathy might never change. She might continue to believe she could drive drunk with no consequences. Eventually, her luck would run out and someone else might pay a heavy price.

I nodded at Fernando and marched toward Cathy's door. Inside her apartment, we gave her a field sobriety test. Not surprisingly, she failed. We cited the proverbial rights, arrested her, and folded her into my police car. All the while she screamed, yelled, and swore that she had not driven her car. I dropped her off at the security detachment on base, ended my shift, and was glad that the entire painful affair was now over.

A month later, I had completely forgotten about the incident. I occasionally saw Cathy on base but did my best to avoid eye contact. Turns out, they wrote up Cathy for driving under the influence, and she now faced court martial charges. Edward informed me that since I had witnessed the situation and had made the arrest, I needed to testify in court.

Military court martial proceedings have some similarities to civilian courts but are far different from what's portrayed on an episode of the *Law & Order* television series. Military commanders can decide arbitrarily whether an offense should be charged at all, as well as in which manner the offenders should be tried or punished. A commander has the discretion to let the matter drop and take no action. This might occur if the case is a bit fuzzy, the circumstances don't warrant action, the evidence is sketchy or inadmissible, or the proceeding might bring harm to the unit or the Air Force in general.

The offense might be light enough that the commander decides to take only administrative rather than punitive action. In this case, the punishment is corrective and rehabilitative, such as a formal reprimand, mandatory counseling, or volunteer work.

The commander can escalate things up a notch by initiating nonjudicial punishment under Article 15 of the Uniform Code of Military Justice (UCMJ). They typically reserve this for minor offenses wherein corrective action needs to be more than just rehabilitation. Nonjudicial punishment hearings are meant to be non-adversarial, consisting of a miniature trial wherein both sides ask a bunch of questions. The commander listens patiently to the answers and asks a few more questions before deciding on a verdict. In these cases, an airman can ask for an open or closed hearing, talk with a military-appointed or civilian attorney (at their own expense), have someone else speak on their behalf, and have witnesses recount what happened. Typical rules of evidence don't apply, and for the airman to be found guilty, the commander must have little doubt that the service member committed the offense. If the commander issues a guilty verdict, the punishment delivered depends on the circumstances and rank of the defendant. The verdict can be appealed, in which case an officer that outranks the issuing commander needs to get involved.

If the offense is bad enough, the commander can opt for a full court martial and then must choose from three different levels: summary, special, or general. These courts martials differ in relation to the rights of the accused, the procedures used, and the levels of punishment that can be assessed.

A summary court martial is the lowest level and is used to deal with minor offenses. Only enlisted personnel can be tried in this way, and only one officer presides over the hearing. The accused airman has no right to counsel, but he or she can use a civilian attorney at their own expense. A special court martial is at the intermediate level and can have only one military judge or at least three jury members and a judge. The accused may ask that at least one-third of the court be comprised of enlisted personnel. For these proceedings, there's a military prosecutor, usually called the trial counsel, and a defense counsel—which can be a military officer or a civilian attorney paid for by the accused.

Finally, a general court martial is the military's highest level, reserved for more serious crimes. This is the most formal, time-con-suming, and difficult proceeding. Punishments can be harsh, albeit up to pre-determined limits. Before any charged crime can be sent to a general court martial, an Article 32 investigation must be com-pleted, which is like a civilian grand jury investigation. At the close of this hearing, an Article 32 officer makes a recommendation on how to proceed, in the same way a civilian judge might decide whether to go to court.

Recommendations aren't binding but are generally followed. At this point, the accused can elect for a trial by a single judge or by a jury with a minimum of five members. Enlisted personnel can opt for a jury with enlisted members comprising one third and officers the other two thirds.

Edward informed me that as this was not Cathy's first DUI, and she had potentially endangered lives more than once, this would be a general court martial. If found guilty, she could receive a bad conduct or dishonorable discharge and lose any accrued retirement benefits. I had attended a few summary and only one special court martial, but this was my first general.

In a general court martial, which is not too dissimilar to a civilian trial, Federal Rules of Evidence must be followed. In this case, much of the evidence lay between my ears. I could not have dismantled Cathy's warm engine hood and placed it in an evidence bag. I did not have pictures of her driving the Toyota. I only had my word and that of a few other witnesses who could only corroborate some of the details. For the most part, the prosecution had to rely on my sworn testimony.

Prior to the trial, I met with the prosecuting attorney, a young Air Force lieutenant named Robert Unger who had limited trial experience. Fortunately, he was sharp and eager and had done a nice job of preparing. He asked me a bunch of questions, drilled me on a few things, and then frowned. I swallowed hard and asked what was wrong.

Lieutenant Unger said that it probably wasn't the best decision to drive Cathy home without another security person present. The defense attorney might drill me on these facts. That said, it was not necessarily related to Cathy's subsequent decision to drive while drunk, so theoretically it should not hold weight. However, the defense might use it to undermine my credibility, and the case might come down to Cathy's word against mine. Feeling like an idiot, I realized that all it had taken was one lapse of judgment to wipe out the "five stars" I'd gotten when my commander had pinned that medal on my chest.

The morning of the trial came, and I was exhausted. Fraught with nervous anticipation, I hadn't slept well the night before. With my heart doing somersaults, I walked into the courtroom—which was small and only had a few desks, tables, and chairs. Behind one table sat the jury. Several observers and witnesses were seated in a row of chairs against one wall. They had set up a desk for the colonel who'd be acting as the judge. He had not yet entered the room. Two additional chairs, currently empty, were reserved for Cathy and her defense counsel. On the opposite side were a desk and several chairs, which were reserved for Bob, the trial counsel, and his witnesses—which included me.

While seated at a desk next to Bob, I turned around and noticed Al and Fernando, the two Portuguese security guys, and Joe the bar bouncer, sitting behind me. All three nodded and smiled. Cathy and her counsel—a military attorney—entered the room and sat at the desk across from us. The room was sparse, and the off-white walls held no pictures. Bright neon bulbs beamed down on my forehead, and my uniform tie felt like a noose as sweat beads formed on my brow.

We all stood at attention when the base commander entered and strode to his seat. He motioned for us to sit and then began the proceedings. I was fascinated by this, as I rarely got to see what happened to the military personnel we apprehended. The defense counsel and trial counsel gave their opening statements. Cathy pleaded not guilty to the charge of violating UCMJ codes by driving drunk.

The defense counsel called me to the stand to testify. My tie fluttered with every heartbeat as I approached and swore to tell the truth. Unlike in the movies, the witness stand consisted of a metal chair inside a small wooden box. I sat and rested my unsteady hands on my knees. When I glanced over at Cathy, she smirked back at me. I didn't understand why until her attorney started drilling me.

He asked me a few questions about how I'd driven Catherine home and why I had done so alone. I answered truthfully. He then asked when I'd started having a relationship with the accused. My eyes widened and my jaw dropped. For a moment, I was tongue-tied and couldn't speak. The attorney asked me again, this time with a more forceful tone. I shook my head and said that I'd never met Catherine before the night of her arrest. The attorney pointed a finger and said that I obviously had previously engaged in an intimate relationship with her that she had ended. Firing more questions, he implied that on the night of her arrest, I tried to get back together with Catherine at the bar, and when she refused, I lied and said she was drunk. I then demanded that I drive her home, which provided me the opportunity to rekindle a relationship with her. I was stunned. I looked over at Bob. He also appeared surprised while frantically rifling through a stack of papers on the table. The defense counsel continued his barrage.

He said witnesses in Catherine's apartment complex confirmed that I had escorted her home. The attorney suggested that I had convinced Fernando, my Portuguese security partner and friend, to join me in lying about Catherine being drunk. He also said I had lied about seeing the defendant driving the Toyota and about the warm vehicle hood.

Finally, Bob voiced an objection and insisted that the defense counsel was fabricating lies. The commanding officer held up a hand to silence the room. He turned and asked me to respond to the accusations.

With my throat constricted, I did my best to tell the truth about what had happened. The commanding officer said that because I did not have a Portuguese security partner with me when I drove Catherine home, the defense counsel had a right to question my motives. Had I not been alone, the accusations might not have held water but now they could not be ignored.

I nodded and lowered my head. They excused me from the stand and then called Fernando to take my place. The defense attorney ripped into him as well, and even though there was a translator to ensure accuracy, the language barrier didn't help. I watched Fernando squirm in his seat and felt my heart sink. This was all my fault, and I felt terrible that he'd been dragged into the fray. The defense counsel called other witnesses, including Joe the bar bouncer and a few of Cathy's neighbors. The trial dragged on for another hour before the defense counsel completed his side of the case. By now it was almost noon, so the commanding officer adjourned the trial until after lunch.

With my stomach churning, I didn't feel like eating, so I downed a bottle of water and took a walk outside. Fernando and Joe met me out front and asked what was going on. They asked if all the accusations were true and if I'd had a relationship with Cathy. Apparently, the defense counsel had done such a good job that even these guys had doubts. I had this terrible feeling that Cathy was going to get off, and I was going to receive judicial punishment in her place.

We walked back into the courtroom and the trial recommenced. The colonel asked Bob to present his case, and the lieutenant appeared befuddled compared to Cathy's attorney. He started off by stuttering, stammering, and struggling to find his notes and documents. He was headed toward a legal cliff and was dragging me down with him. My stomach churned, and I felt nauseated.

Finally, the commanding officer, acting as the judge, interrupted and asked Bob a few questions. I could tell that he was tacitly trying to help guide Bob along. Fortunately, it worked. Bob gained more confidence and momentum. He started doing a fine job of undermining the notion that I'd previously had a relationship with Catherine and therefore had no motive to perpetrate a series of lies. He called me to the stand to clarify the facts, and through his questioning, showed there was no evidence I'd been dating the defendant and no indication that I'd convinced Fernando or Joe to lie about the facts. Catherine was obviously drunk at the bar, as later verified by a field sobriety test, and I'd driven her home as ordered. Al would have joined me if it hadn't been the end of our shift. Fernando had no motive to lie about the warm Toyota hood. Bob then brought up my exemplary service and the commendation medal I'd received a few months earlier.

Bob called a few more people to the stand but did not take as long as the defense counsel to present his case. He gave his closing remarks, followed by the defense attorney, and then the base commander instructed the jury to leave the room and determine a verdict.

During the break, I again went outside, but this time chose not to talk with anyone. I was too nervous. My career was on the line. While I wasn't on trial yet, if the verdict came back not guilty, I might soon face my own court martial.

They called us back in, and we took our seats. My chest felt heavy, as if I'd been wrapped in duct tape. We stood as the jury entered the room along with the judge. The jury sat, except for one member who remained standing. His perfectly pressed uniform displayed a row of ribbons above his left pocket. The commander asked if the jury had reached a verdict, and the officer said they had. The commander asked the officer to read the verdict.

I held my breath and uttered a silent prayer.

Guilty.

I breathed out a long sigh. Bob pumped a silent fist into the air. I glanced over at Catherine. She glared back at me while an officer ushered her out of the room. I later learned that she appealed the verdict but was denied. I was told that during the proceeding she apparently used several expletives in front of a brigadier general. He got angry and demoted her on the spot. I also heard she eventually received a bad conduct discharge, but as this information was relayed secondhand, it could not be verified.

I also learned something quite valuable from this experience: balance. There's a time to cut corners or bend rules, such as with the lieutenant who ran from us during the fake arrest for the charity fundraiser. On the flip side, there's a time when not taking proper precautions can be costly or even devastating. By making a few rookie mistakes at the wrong time, I had almost ruined my career, and possibly the careers and reputations of others. That day, as I walked away from the courtroom, I made a commitment to myself and to the Air Force. From that moment forward, I'd wear my uniform with pride and take my job more seriously. Others were counting on me to protect them, and I did not want to let them down.

I spent fifteen months in the Azores before receiving orders to report to a new command in Italy. I was sad to be leaving paradise but excited about what lay beyond the next horizon.

CHAPTER 8:

THE ABDUCTION

What lay beyond the next horizon was pizza. In the summer of 2008, I bid farewell to the sandy beaches, amazing seafood, and friendly residents of the Azores—also, cold bottles of Sagres beer. I flew home to the United States for a month to visit my family and friends and reminisce about what it was like to be a civilian. As an E-4 in the Air Force, I had no regrets about my enlistment decision and felt as much at home in the military as I did in my parent's home. I had two families now, and I looked forward to spending time with both.

I enjoyed my vacation Stateside, but I was also excited about starting my next adventure in Europe. The Air Force had sent me to the Aviano Air Base in Italy. I had read about the area, but printed words and static photos always pale in comparison to the real thing. I completed the long journey overseas and reported to my new command in June.

The Aviano Air Base is nestled near the base of the Dolomite Mountains in the beautiful northern region of Friuli-Venezia Giulia, and at the time it was home to the 31st Fighter Wing of F-16 aircraft. The Italian *Aeronautica Militare* built the airbase in 1911 and still has jurisdiction over the area, but not over the base. During World War I, the Italians used the runways to launch air raids over Germany and then switched sides in World War II to fly missions against Allied forces. The British captured the field in 1945 and turned it over to the U.S. Air Force in 1954.

When I arrived at the base, I noticed that some buildings appeared old while others displayed patches of new construction. The base is rooted in rich history and historic involvement. In June 1995, during the Bosnia conflict, the 555th Fighter Squadron undertook a massive search and rescue mission to find and retrieve a downed pilot, Captain Scott O'Grady, after he'd evaded capture for almost a week.

The Thirty-First has been involved in several more conflicts since then in the Balkans, Serbia, Kosovo, Kuwait, and Operation Iraqi Freedom in 2003. Over the years, fighter squadrons operating from Aviano have flown thousands of combat sorties in the region. In 2008, there were over 10,000 military and civilian personnel stationed at Aviano supporting the 31st Fighter Wing, which was made up of four groups. The operations group is responsible for ensuring combat readiness for two F-16CG squadrons. One is an air control squadron and the other an operational support squadron. Together they train, equip, and plan missions while providing weather, intelligence, evaluation, and command for all flying operations.

The maintenance group does all the heavy lifting and bolt tightening to keep the planes flying, and the mission support group provides infrastructure and service to support the capability and quality of life of the airmen and pilots. The medical group gives you a lollipop after sewing up a laceration or pulling a tooth and ensures your vaccination shots are up to date.

Given the mission parameters and the types of weapons stored at the base—which included conventional and non-conventional—I knew my job at Aviano would be far different and more demanding than it had been in the Azores. I had graduated from being a street cop and was now a full-fledged security airman. Part of me looked forward to stepping up to a new and more demanding role, but part of me knew that I'd first need to endure several months of difficult freshman training again.

Fortunately, I had an excellent instructor. Technical Sergeant John Smith was a former training instructor and became my mentor and boss. He stood erect and tall, and his short, brown hair was always trimmed to perfect standards. His shoes were polished to a radiant shine and his uniform neatly pressed. He took me under his wing and taught me how to play by the rules and take pride in my job. He was a do-it-right kind of guy with a strong moral compass, but like my former bosses in the Azores, he always took care of his people.

John was strict, and made you drop and do pushups if you were a minute late for muster, but I admired and respected his attention to detail and by-the-book military demeanor. During my first month on the base, after long hours of drills and practice, they allowed me to make my first patrol alongside another new guy named Sam Norton. My sidekick was a jovial guy with chipmunk cheeks. Sam had a bright personality but also tended to get distracted and make mistakes now and then. We were both excited about conducting our first patrol, and I wanted to show my boss, John, that he could trust me to complete the assignment properly. Unfortunately, things didn't work out as planned.

Our job entailed responding to building alarms or threat alerts within a specific amount of time, usually under three minutes, and approaching the facility or location in the proper manner. We weren't allowed to use a GPS to plan our routes because they required us to memorize the location of every street and structure. When our first alert came in, my heart pounded with excitement. I set a timer on my watch and pointed straight ahead. Sam gunned the engine, and our military armored vehicle jolted forward. He had wide eyes, and his hands were tightly wrapped about the steering wheel while tapping one finger as he raced around corners. Even though I gave him clear instructions regarding which route to take, he repeatedly made wrong turns and zigged instead of zagged. I looked at my watch and a lump formed in my throat. We had less than a minute left, and we were nowhere near our destination. I advised Sam to speed up so we'd make it on time. That was a mistake. Sam got even more flustered and made even more wrong turns. By the time we found the building, we were over three minutes late—twice the allotted time.

John was furious. He pointed a long finger and fumed. If this had been an actual incident, lives could have been lost. We had failed our first assignment. It didn't matter that Sam had steered wrong, we were a team and should have practiced more diligently. We should have spent more time memorizing routes and simulating alert calls. We thought we were ready, but we weren't. I decided that day to practice my assignments more meticulously until I could find my way blindfolded. I prayed that I'd never be thrusted into a situation where my actions could determine if someone lived or died, but if thrown into the proverbial fire, I didn't want anyone to pay the ultimate price for my mistakes.

Later that same day, as punishment for our failure, John made us do the exercise again several more times. Only on these runs, he made us park over a mile away, don our gear and gas masks, run at a brisk clip to the building, and then clamber up a tall flight of stairs. By the end of our fourth simulated incident, my face was flushed from fatigue and my legs felt like putty. That night, after my weary head hit the pillow, I effortlessly logged in ten hours of sleep.

When not responding to building alarms, we patrolled taxiways and aircraft storage areas to prevent theft, sabotage, or criminal activity. Occasionally, we drove off base to deal with incidents, accidents, or family fights involving American base personnel. While the Italians maintained area jurisdiction, they relied on us to police our own. Occasionally, the locals lent us a hand. One rainy night, dispatchers sent Sam and me to the scene of a car accident involving the wife of an Air Force pilot. A thunderous storm had coated the streets with slick sheets of water and made driving almost impossible. The pilot's wife had skidded off the edge of the road and careened into a deep ravine. Sam and I helped the woman up the side of the ditch and ushered her into an ambulance. She was shaken but otherwise fine.

We went back to our vehicle, and while sitting in the front seat and struggling to fill out our paperwork in the dim light, an Italian man in a nearby home came out in a raincoat. He tapped on the window, and in broken English, invited us into his house. In the compact kitchen, the man's wife made us warm soup and lasagna Bolognese. We were stunned but grateful. Most of the locals were like that—friendly and inviting. They helped make my time in Aviano memorable and rewarding.

John was a tough boss, but I eventually flourished under his leadership. Mistakes were corrected, but when we did our job right, he rewarded us. Sometimes the rewards included the most delicious pizza I'd ever eaten. John had discovered a quaint restaurant near the base, and while they didn't serve Sagres beer, they offered an admirable substitute with Italian-made Peroni. Aviano had a town square lined with a variety of shops, bakeries, and cafes that served European cappuccino and homemade gelato. On the weekends, merchants set up dozens of tables to display fresh fruit, pasta, and carved meat. Above the rooftops, we could see the snow-covered peaks of the Dolomite Mountains—less than twenty minutes away by car.

The town church, Chiesa di San Zenone, is stunning. When a few of us visited the structure, we stood in awe while gazing at the intricate designs and architectural craftsmanship that attracts thousands of tourists each year. Just outside Aviano, we explored the Sorgente del Gorgazzo, an underwater cave that sparkles with shimmering blue water. We also strolled through a canopy of green and auburn at St Florian's Rural Park.

The Friuli-Venezia Giulia, where Aviano is situated, comprises one of Italy's twenty regions. At the time, it was home to over a million residents, and many of them lived in the capital port town of Trieste. During my first few months at the base, some of us drove out to the seaside city to explore the grand piazza and narrow streets lined with bright green- and pink-painted apartments. Above our heads, colorful garments hung on clotheslines and flapped in the breeze. On the shores of the Gulf, Trieste's Castello di Miramare is a marvel of creative genius and one of the most striking buildings in all of Italy.

Venice also became a favorite place to visit by train from Aviano. It's famous for gondolas gliding along narrow canals, apartments splashed with an array of pastels, and culinary delights on every street corner. I found something new and exciting every time I visited—which was often. During my time in Aviano, I went to Venice at least a dozen times and came back several pounds heavier. I also spent many hours walking the labyrinth streets of Florence while admiring ancient statues, manicured gardens, and ornate structures. Rome and Naples were also accessible by train, and many of us were in awe as we wandered around the busy streets and visited famous landmarks such as the Colosseum, where gladiators once battled in front of cheering crowds.

By train, the Austrian town of Villach was only a few hours away from the base. Known for its luxurious thermal baths and the brilliant blue Lake Faak, you can spend hours walking along wooded paths near dozens of rivers or browsing quaint shops in the village. The Austrian people were always open and talkative, and I felt welcome every time I visited the region. When time didn't permit longer trips, some of us visited the Piancavallo ski resort in the Dolomite Mountain range. This frosty area offers over ten miles of pristine ski slopes that attract visitors from across Europe. During the summer, the Dolomites also feature many miles of hiking trails where nature lovers can spot goat-antelope hybrids called chamois or large-horned sheep known as mouflon.

Kočevje, Slovenia is also only a few hours away from Aviano. Surrounded by preserved primeval forests and riddled with cold streams, Kočevje offers some of the best nature hikes in Europe. I was mesmerized by the historical and artistic treasures found in this elegant European locale. The crumbling remains of Friedrichstein Castle reminded me of the tragic love story between Veronika of Desenice and Frederick of Celje that took place there. During our visit, my colleagues and I sampled the local cuisine and craft brews and then wandered the narrow streets of the small town. We walked across a stone bridge and tossed coins into the clear stream. Near the end of the day, we clambered back into my car and drove toward the border.

At the Slovenian border station, a tall guard in a gray uniform held up a hand. I rolled to a stop. The guard motioned for me to pull out of the line and park near a small building. I glanced at my friends and shrugged. Once parked, the guard came over and tried to speak English. He had to repeat his questions several times before I nodded. I thought he wanted to see my vehicle registration, which I handed him. He called for another police officer, who strolled over and studied the document. The two conversed rapidly while pointing at the paper.

Finally, the other guard bent down and peered through my rolled-down window. He had a stern face and angry eyes. He pointed at my windshield and asked a question. I had no idea what he was saying. His partner called over and mouthed the English word "sticker." The stern guy nodded, pointed again, and said "sticker." I still did not know what he wanted. After several more minutes of explanation using fractured English, my eyes widened. They were fining us the equivalent of 300 USD because we didn't have a Slovenian registration sticker on the windshield. Apparently, unbeknownst to us, we should have gotten one on our way into the country. As an E-4 in the Air Force, $300 was no small sum. I argued with the guards but lost the battle. The four of us scraped together enough cash to pay the fine, which I suspect the two guys pocketed. Lesson learned. Google before driving across foreign borders.

By 2009, when I drove across a German border to visit Ramstein, the massive Air Force base was home to over 50,000 American service members and 5,000 U.S. civilian employees. Ramstein is in the German state of Rheinland-Pfalz and is part of the Kaiserslautern—the largest American military community outside the U.S. The area was nothing more than a huge swamp back in World War II. In 1948, U.S. and French occupational forces agreed to build a train line from Einsiedlerhof to Kaiserslautern to haul in loads of dirt and create a raised, smooth surface. They then constructed two airbases, which took three years and 270,000 workers to complete. The base also employed around 6,000 German workers and 16,000 contractors from several countries. It's one of the largest airbases in the world, which could make it a target for terrorists. I was excited about exploring Germany, but I was also painfully aware that whenever I was in uniform, I'd also be a potential target. I changed into civilian clothes before venturing off base.

Frankfurt is known for its advanced engineering and modern cityscape. While I didn't visit the civilian airport on that trip to Germany, I knew it was one of the busiest in the world, on par with any of the New York airports. On the river Main and featuring the headquarters for the Frankfurt Stock Exchange and European Central Bank, the city is considered as the transportation center of Germany and the financial capital of continental Europe.

Prior to the Second World War, Frankfurt was famous for having the largest timber-framed old town in Europe. After the war, the Germans rebuilt the Römerberg area, which later became a popular spot for tourists seeking unique ornaments and gifts at winter Christmas markets. In sharp contrast to the forests of Slovenia, Frankfurt has become so large that it's often referred to as "Mainhattan," but given the plethora of financial institutions, some also call it "Bankfurt."

I called it amazing while gawking at the skyline with my head tilted back and mouth half open. I walked the streets and met dozens of friendly people, who all spoke excellent English. Along the way, I learned six things I should never do in Germany: Jaywalk, lest you want to get arrested. They're pretty serious about that. Never walk on a bicycle lane. They're even more strict about that. Don't point a finger at your head, it means you think the other person is crazy. Don't chew gum. I guess it makes you look like you're from New Jersey. Don't place your hand in a pocket while talking. Maybe they think you're reaching for a pack of gum. And finally, take your shoes off before entering someone's home. They prefer stinky feet to dirty floors.

All joking aside, I found the German people to be warm and welcoming and I enjoyed every minute of my time there. I was looking forward to coming back soon and staying for more than a weekend. Little did I know that my next visit would not be so glorious.

A year and a half after my arrival in Aviano, after I'd finally settled in and had become proficient at my new job, something unexpected rocked our world. On November 4, 2009, an Italian court convicted twenty-two U.S. CIA agents, an Air Force colonel, and two Italian SISMI secret agents for their role in the kidnapping of Hassan Mustafa Osama Nasr on February 17, 2003. I had heard about the incident, which had been called the "extraordinary rendition" program, but only knew a few sparse details. After the conviction, the topic became an all-consuming lunch conversation, and I became privy to more inside information from some officers who'd been on the base at the time. They said Nasr had been captured in Milan by CIA agents and taken to the Aviano Air Base for interrogation. They then transported him to the Ramstein Air Base in Germany and then to Alexandria, Egypt, where they turned him over to Egypt's State Security Investigation (SSI) force.

I learned that in 2001, Nasr was a radical Egyptian cleric and possibly part of the infamous al-Gama'a al-Islamiyya. When that organization came under scrutiny by the Egyptian government for terrorist activities, Nasr fled to Italy, where they granted him political asylum. In early 2002, Italian and American intelligence agencies started looking into Nasr's activities. They set up electronic surveillance and wiretapped his phone. Eventually, the Italians dug up evidence of Nasr's connections to al-Qaeda. They also believed he was secretly building a network to recruit and support terrorists. They found a trail of breadcrumbs that led to Ansar al-Islam, a terrorist group that had been training and shuttling combatants to Iraqi Kurdistan. The Americans, working with the Italians, also suspected that Nasr was involved in a plot to attack the U.S. embassy in Rome, as well as blow up the American School of Milan, which housed the children of several foreign diplomats.

On February 17, 2003, a month prior to the invasion of Iraq, Hassan Mustafa Osama Nasr was walking toward a mosque in Milan to complete his noon prayers. Several CIA agents shoved him into a black minivan on Via Giuseppe Guerzoni. They covered his head with a bag and drove him to the Aviano Air Base, about five hours away. Allegedly, the CIA took him to an interrogation room in Area E and questioned him for several hours. They then flew him by Learjet, using the call sign SPAR 92 (which stands for Special Air Resources, an airlift transport service for VIPs), to the Ramstein Airbase in Germany. There, the CIA turned him over to the German authorities. The Germans were not happy about the nature of Nasr's arrest and launched an official investigation into the matter. Not surprisingly, they weren't able to find much evidence against the CIA and eventually dropped the case. Nasr was later flown to Cairo, where they threw him into prison.

By April 2004, after the dust had settled on the Iraq War, they downgraded Nasr's incarceration a few levels from "potentially dangerous terrorist" to "just a possible bad guy." The authorities moved him from the prison and placed him under house arrest, where he made several phone calls to his friends and family in Egypt. He told them how he'd been taken by Egypt's SSI unit and sent to the Tora prison where he'd been mistreated. Unaware that his calls were being monitored, Nasr was again dragged away and thrown back into prison for his dissidence.

The supposed terrorist spent another three years behind bars before again being released on February 11, 2007. An Egyptian court ruled that his imprisonment had been unfounded, but Nasr received no reparations. Cellphone records obtained by the police department in Milan later implicated the twenty-two CIA agents originally involved in the abduction. The agents had not removed the batteries from their phones, which allowed the police to use GPS tracking to reconstruct their movements over a nine-day period. During that time, the agents had made several calls to the U.S. consulate in Milan, as well as the CIA headquarters in Virginia.

Robert Seldon Lady, a former CIA chief stationed in Milan, had led the CIA operation. Under diplomatic cover as the consul of the U.S., he had been operating from the Milan U.S. embassy and working with the CIA's Special Activities Division. Lady later admitted that he'd opposed Nasr's abduction but had been overruled.

In June 2005, Italian judge Guido Salvini issued arrest warrants for the twenty-two CIA agents, including Jeffrey W. Castelli, who had been the head of the CIA in Italy during the incident. Salvini said the abduction violated international law and was therefore illegal. In a contradictory move, he also charged Nasr with acts of terrorism and issued a warrant for his arrest.

The CIA argued that the Italian government obviously believed Nasr was a terrorist and was aware of and complicit in his arrest. They offered ample evidence to support their claim. The entire affair smoldered for years until November 2009, when an Italian judge convicted—in absentia—the twenty-two CIA agents and the two Italian agents. They sentenced the former Milan CIA chief, Robert Lady, to eight years in prison. The other agents received five-year sentences. They were also ordered to pay hefty reparations to Nasr and his wife. A U.S. Pentagon official said the case held no merit and none of the convicted CIA agents were extradited. In the end, only a few Italians ever served time and the high-profile incident faded away.

After the meaningless conviction in late 2009, I wondered if the affair might spark revenge by the Taliban or other terrorist groups, or empower them to recruit more young Muslims and turn them toward the dark side. I was concerned that the incident might eventually spur counterattacks against U.S. military personnel.

Less than a year and a half later, my fears became reality.

CHAPTER 9:

THE JOURNEY

My heart skipped a beat as I scanned my small dorm room for the last time and then bid farewell to Margherita pizzas and spaghetti Bolognese. In early June 2010, it was time to leave Italy and report to my new command in the United Kingdom. I flew home for a month to visit my family and then boarded a plane bound for Gatwick Airport in England. I'd visited the UK a few times with my family prior to joining the military as my dad's relatives are from Wales. I recalled marveling at the vast countryside in that area, covered with blankets of green and yellow. As a young boy, my eyes widened at the sight of Guernsey cows and horned goats grazing in the hayfields. The Welsh love their food and were always offering me tasty scones covered with clotted cream. I was in heaven.

My friend Amber, who I'd trained with in the Azores, was stationed at Mildenhall—a Royal Air Force Base near Lakenheath. She met me at the terminal and gave me a ride. Not yet used to being on the left side of the road, I gripped the edges of my seat as Amber careened around corners and sped through yellow lights. We reminisced about our time in the Azores while she gave me a brief tour of the area. An hour later, we arrived at the outskirts of Lakenheath village. The town is in the West Suffolk district of eastern England, and at the time, the population was less than 5,000. Nestled next to the Fens and Breckland, those living in the area enjoy a country lifestyle along the borders of two wildlife playgrounds painted by Mother Nature. The Brits created Lakenheath Fen Nature Reserve in 1996 to restore wetlands decimated by carrot-growing agricultural fields. The local residents were ecstatic, but the rabbits weren't.

The village is spectacular, featuring a Victorian primary school built in 1878 and a small main street lined with a variety of shops, pubs, and tea houses. There are also a few parks where children play soccer in the summer and skate on frozen ponds in the winter.

Lakenheath is best known for its medieval church, built around 900 years ago using wood and then later remodeled with local flint. Outside, the religious structure features an embattled parapet with a line of evil-looking gargoyles and other strangely carved creatures. I'd only had one beer on my flight, so I wasn't worried about being mauled to death by a gargoyle for my sins, but I still wished I was wearing my sidearm. Inside, the tall pillars held up an ornate ceiling that melted into walls covered with stained glass windows, dark medieval paintings, and religious carvings on the pews. On the faces of the church's carved wooden angels, deep scars reflected memories of the English Civil War.

Back on the road, Amber drove us past a recently built pavilion she said housed the local cricket club and hosted various events. Lakenheath apparently also has a football (soccer) club that plays in the town's stadium. We cruised through a few neighborhoods and past rustic fences bordering several farms, and then Amber pointed her front grill toward the air base.

The Royal Air Force (RAF) Lakenheath Air Base is home to the largest deployment of U.S. Air Force personnel in the UK. The U.S. has occupied the airfield since the first bombers flew in during World War II to conduct air raids on Germany. Despite the UK RAF designation, over 6,000 U.S. Air Force personnel occupy the base, which is part of the 48th Fighter Wing.

The Brits started using the airfield during World War I as an area for bi-wing planes to practice dropping bombs and strafing enemy troops. After the war, in 1918, the RAF abandoned Lakenheath and then brought it back to life in 1940 as a decoy to minimize attacks against nearby RAF Mildenhall. The British used fake runways, planes, and landing lights to trick the German Luftwaffe into attacking an empty base instead of Mildenhall. Later during the war, they turned it into an actual working airfield to serve as a backup to Mildenhall. Short Stirling bombers and a squadron of Vickers Wellingtons rumbled onto newly paved runways and took part in more than 350 wartime operations against Germany.

As we pulled up to the Lakenheath gate, I remembered reading about the story of one Stirling pilot during World War II. On the night of November 28, 1942, Flight Sergeant Rawdon Middleton suffered serious face and body wounds from shells fired during a raid on the Fiat manufacturing site in Turin, Italy. Despite a massive loss of blood and subsequent delirium from his wounds, he fought to guide his aircraft safely back to Lakenheath, where his crew bailed out and were rescued. Middleton crashed his Stirling into the English Channel and was posthumously awarded the Victoria Cross for his valor.

I shuddered at the thought of how dozens of similar incidents had occurred during the war and how many other brave souls had been lost to keep England free from tyranny. I felt privileged to have been given the opportunity to carry on the legacy and do my part to keep the world safe from terrorists and dictators who might force suffering and death on others.

Toward the end of the war, in 1945, they constructed new runways at Lakenheath to make way for U.S. Air Force Boeing B-29 Superfortress and B-24 Liberator bombers. The war ended before they completed the work, and the base sat empty until the Cold War started in 1947. At that time, to support training exercises, President Harry S. Truman ordered Strategic Air Command (SAC) B-29 bombers to RAF Burtonwood in Lancashire, as well as to a few bases in West Germany. The exercises were ruses as Truman's real agenda was to establish a permanent home in the UK and Germany for the B-29s to counter threats from the Soviets. To support that goal, they sent B-29s to Lakenheath in 1948 on a three-month temporary deployment. The B-29s remained there, however, and control of the base was transferred to the U.S. Air Force in early 1950. Over the years, the type of aircraft stationed at the airbase changed with the times, but the mission objectives remained unchanged during the Cold War, and that mission included the handling of unconventional weapons.

This posture eventually led to two serious incidents.

The first occurred on July 27, 1956, when a B-47 bomber crashed into a storage igloo that held three Mark-6 unconventional weapons. The plane exploded, showering the igloo with burning fuel. Even though the Mark-6 bombs inside didn't have any plutonium fissile cores installed, they did contain depleted uranium-238. Fortunately, the base personnel quelled the fire before the bombs exploded, but

I imagined that during the close call, there were dozens of worried faces and sweat-drenched foreheads. Afterward, one bomb disposal expert said it was nothing short of a miracle that the exposed detonators on one bomb didn't explode and cause a disaster. However, sadly, four of the B-47's crew died in the accident.

Naturally, the Brits were quite concerned about the event as it interrupted their teatime. That, and it nearly caused public panic as U.S. authorities overstepped boundaries and called for evacuations in the region. The British government decided it best to enact a new policy in the future. Should a bomb accidentally fall into a haystack on an English countryside, and the press got wind of it, the government would handle the incident without alerting the public. Keep calm and carry on. Tallyho and all that, mate. Please ignore that mushroom cloud and pass the scones.

The tactic worked well for five years, as nothing out of the ordinary happened until January 1961. Then, a U.S. Air Force F-100 Super Sabre parked at Lakenheath caught fire after a pilot accidentally jettisoned his fuel tanks. The metal containers clanked onto the concrete tarmac, ruptured, and cracked open. The aviation fuel ignited and engulfed the plane in flames. Inside, a Mark-28 hydrogen bomb started to sweat. Response teams also started sweating as they raced to douse the fire before the bomb's arming components triggered and the high explosives detonated. This time, the U.S. issued no evacuation warnings to the locals, not that it mattered. If the bomb had gone off, few would have been able to get far enough away in time. Air Force personnel finally put out the fire, and no one had been hurt or killed.

After the incident, not much exciting happened at Lakenheath for a few decades. Then, in 1986, several F-111 bombers from the 48th Tactical Fighter Wing dropped conventional bombs on Muammar

Gaddafi's head in Libya. The bombers missed Gaddafi but did destroy several military targets. The mission spurred the mock-acronym for Libya: Lakenheath Is Bombing Your Ass. Unfortunately, the Libyans did shoot down one F-111, and two pilots died.

I reported to my new squadron at Lakenheath as an E-4 senior airman and soon discovered that this was going to be the most challenging duty assignment of my Air Force career. I spent the first week getting oriented and meeting my new boss. His name was Joe Nelson, and as a seasoned E-5 staff sergeant, he knew his stuff. He was very patient, analytical, and articulate; he broke down my training into manageable bite-sized chunks. He was demanding and critical but also encouraging and understanding. He called me on my mistakes but then took the time to walk me through what I'd done wrong and how to do it correctly.

Ten days after arriving at Lakenheath, the Air Force promoted me to an E-5 staff sergeant, which meant I could now afford to live off base. They also gave me some time off to find a place. I did some house hunting in a small nearby village called Beck Row. The rural town consisted mainly of small row houses connected by walls. I found and rented one that was joined to four other homes, and fortunately all my neighbors were friendly. A few of them were American airmen, like me, including Brad Hazelton and his wife, Sarah. They lived a few doors down from me and often invited me over for dinner. We shared stories about our military experiences and then played cards or watched a movie. Brad was a staff sergeant at Lakenheath and gave me several pointers about getting around, who does what, and most importantly, who to avoid. Brad said there were always a few individuals who were challenged by life, and it was best to not inadvertently make their day…or mine…even worse.

Beck Row didn't have a typical main street but had a few shops and a great pub around the corner from my flat called the Rose and Crown. Given that it was only a five-minute walk, it didn't take me long to develop a fondness for English beer and Sunday roasts. The latter is a tradition in the UK. Seems like everyone gets excited about going to the local pub on Sunday to indulge in Yorkshire pudding, beets, and roast beef and pork. I had to double my exercise routine to keep the pounds off.

My unit on the base was heavily involved in law enforcement, aircraft security, and base defense. Within my first few months, I completed my certification as a controller—qualified in maintaining base security—and they assigned me to the Base Defense Operations Center. My duties entailed taking 911 calls, dispatching patrols, and coordinating with various teams to respond to incidents, such as a fire or potential threat. After the 2005 terrorist bombing of a bus in London, the "brass" senior officers on the base had become concerned about terrorist threats.

Fortunately, no terrorists attacked Lakenheath during my tour of duty, but one incident in London sent us into a high-alert status. Apparently, a man attacked a British soldier who was wearing a Help for Heroes shirt. Given the nature of the incident, our command took no chances. Heightened security measures were implemented as a result.

After the attack, many of us befriended our British military counterparts. Since I was ancestrally a Welsh American, I formed a few close friendships with some of the British guards on the base. Even though they were civilians, they worked for the Ministry of Defence and had received military training to maintain base security. We frequented the Rose and Crown together for a pint and swapped security stories. I discovered we shared a lot of the same values and dedication to duty.

I also spent time with Senior Airman Kevin Ortiz at the homes of our mutual friends. He and I worked together and often downed a pint after hours. Kevin was a jovial guy of Hispanic descent with dark hair and brown eyes. He had an adventurous spirit and was always playfully slapping someone on the back. He was outgoing, optimistic, and loved the Air Force. Originally from Texas, Kevin had polite, soft-spoken, and helpful personality.

I also befriended Senior Airman Nick Alden, who had sandy blond hair and stood about five-feet-nine-inches tall. Nick wasn't overly muscular but was a toned 190 pounds and displayed a lot of stamina. He had volunteered to be a machine-gunner, which is no easy task. The M240B gas-operated guns are heavy, weighing almost twenty-eight pounds. Lugging one around for hours takes a lot of endurance. Nick loved the job and took pride in hitting his targets and completing training missions successfully. He rarely complained and liked to set lofty stretch goals for himself.

Nick had transferred to Lakenheath about a year earlier in October 2010 and brought his wife with him from his previous duty station in Alaska. Nick often joked that the UK was the only place in the world with colder weather than Alaska. He and his wife had two children who they adored.

Nick hailed from Anderson, South Carolina. Although his voice displayed only the barest hint of an accent, his manners were definitely Southern. Nick was deeply religious and treated his wife and kids like gold. I could tell they always came first in his life. They seemed happy and content and gave me hope that I'd someday enjoy a similar family life filled with smiles.

Occasionally, when given a bit more time off, I traveled to Wales to visit my relatives. They were always excited to see me and stuffed me full of tea and Welsh cakes. I never understood the beans slapped on bread thing, but they went down well with a side of eggs. Back on the base, I continued my dispatch duties and learned more about Air Force security procedures. While my job was interesting and satisfying, I didn't feel like I was fulfilling the passion and purpose that had propelled me to enlist in the military. One day, while drinking English tea and staring out the window of my small home, I recalled how I'd felt on 9/11. I remembered how that day had changed my life. It had infused me with a desire to serve and protect and ensure something like that would never happened again. The conviction I'd felt over the years after 9/11 welled up inside me once more. I wanted to make a difference, but I wasn't sure how. I got on my knees and ask for guidance.

The next day, I received an answer.

My boss, Joe, called me into his office. A lump formed in my throat as I was certain I was about to be yelled at for making a mistake. Joe motioned for me to sit. I did and forced myself to remain calm. If I'd screwed up, I decided I just needed to take the blow, understand what I'd done wrong, and focus on getting it right the next time.

Joe cleared his throat and reached for a folder on his desk. He opened it and rifled through some pages. Not sure where he was headed, I nodded and said nothing. Joe then mentioned a term called "dwell time." I'd heard of this but wasn't exactly sure what it meant. He explained that for all branches of the military, dwell time refers to the number of months service members spend in a home or non-combat station before being deployed. The term is used to calculate what's called a deploy-to-dwell ratio, which allows personnel an appropriate mental and physical break between combat deployments. The ratio used to be longer, but after 9/11, it had been reduced. So far, I'd spent my entire four-year enlistment in non-combat duty stations, and it was now my turn to deploy.

While sitting in front of Joe's desk, my throat felt parched, and I had trouble replying. Although my mouth was dry, I squeaked out a question and asked where I was headed. Joe leaned back in his chair. His brow furled, and in his eyes I saw a combination of sympathy and concern. He blew out a long breath and said I was going to Afghanistan.

A jolt of adrenaline shot through my body. Had I heard him right? At that time, the war there was at a peak. Body bags were being loaded into transport planes daily. There were no safe corners for U.S. military personnel serving in that region. Every local you met there might want you dead, and every piece of trash on the side of a road could hide an IED.

Joe said I had orders to report to Kandahar Airfield, smack dab in the middle of the bloodiest war zone. I'd be working for the Joint Defense Operations Center as an intel liaison. This was not a traditional role for security services personnel, so prior to my deployment, I'd need to spend several weeks training with my team in Germany and then a few more weeks at a Force Protection Intelligence school at Fort Dix in New Jersey. My understanding of terrorism was about to change in ways I could never have imagined.

Joe also informed me that given my rank, training, and experience, I'd been selected as a leader for some members on the team deploying with me to Afghanistan. I'd now have a few airmen reporting to me and needed to hone my leadership skills. During our time in Afghanistan, they'd be relying on me to keep them alert and alive. I rubbed my hands together and prayed that I was up to the task. I also prayed that I'd make it back alive from my first deployment to a war zone.

This is the Fallen Defender Memorial at RAF Lakenheath. It is in honor of SrA Jason Nathan and SrA Nicholas Alden. It was dedicated on March 2, 2012—one year after the shooting in Frankfurt.

This is a group photo that was taken in January of 2011 in Baumholder, Germany. This was during pre-deployment training for Afghanistan. SrA Nicholas Alden is on the far right. Trevor is third from the right standing up.

A patriotic citizen holds a sign during the funeral
procession for SrA Nicholas Alden.

SrA Nicholas Alden's casket is carried into place during a
memorial ceremony in Anderson, South Carolina.

SrA Nicholas Alden's casket is carried into place during a
memorial ceremony in Anderson, South Carolina.

General Norton Schwartz, Air Force Chief of Staff, presented
Trevor the Airman's Medal on February 9, 2012 at RAF Lakenheath.
Arid Uka was sentenced to life in prison the same day.

From left to right, Air Force Chief of Staff Norton Schwartz, Trevor's mom, Diana Brewer, Trevor, Trevor's dad Donald Brewer, during an awards ceremony at RAF Lakeneheath on February 11, 2012.

From left to right, US Ambassador to Germany Phillip Murphy, Mr. Lamar Conner (helped translate and chased Arid Uka as well), Trevor, and Interior Minister Hans-Peter Friedrich, in Berlin, Germany at the Ministry of the Interior.

Trevor accepting the Order of the Cross of Merit from the
Interior Minister in Berlin. The Order of the Cross of Merit
is the highest award given to a non-German citizen.

Posing for a photo with the US Ambassador to Germany, Phillip Murphy.

Shaking hands with Phillip Murphy, the US Ambassador to Germany.

Talking with the Interior Minister after the medal
presentation ceremony in Berlin.

CHAPTER 10:

TRAINING FOR WAR

In early January 2011, along with several members on the team I'd be serving with in Afghanistan, I climbed aboard a bus headed for Baumholder Air Base in Germany for our pre-deployment training. The ride was a long twelve hours in an Air Force bus across rural UK and German countrysides. We slept most of the way, but when awake, I took time to get to know everyone.

Reginald Carter was a tall, black gentleman with a quiet, calm demeanor and a warm smile. He spoke with a soft, deep baritone that made him sound like an announcer on a jazz radio station. He'd have a beer along with the rest of us, but he never went too far. He always followed protocol and rarely drew outside the lines. He was a consummate perfectionist with a strong moral compass.

Brandon Delaney was a short, wiry guy and only nineteen years old. Being smaller and younger, he was somewhat timid and often got picked on by others. He took it in stride, shrugged it off, and maintained a good sense of humor. Most of the time the barbs thrown his way were playful and mild, but if someone jabbed too hard, I some-times felt obligated to step in and shut it down. Being a bit on the smaller side myself, I recalled the beating I'd taken in the boy's room in high school and commiserated with the underdogs.

Brandon was always eager to fit in and not be left out of any group activities, whether in the field during training or after hours when having a beer at the enlisted club. He was loyal, intelligent, and bit high strung but also jovial and likable. He'd always try to laugh off the social spears thrown his way, but I often saw him recoil and wince. I could tell that the insults bothered him. He reminded me of the typical small kid on the playground that becomes the punching bag for bullies. Regardless, I respected Brandon as I knew he was also destined to serve in Afghanistan, albeit at a different base. While some of us were headed to Kandahar, he and a few others were going to Bagram Airfield.

Nick Alden, who I knew well already, was more introverted than extroverted but opened up a lot more during our long bus ride. He mostly talked about his family while sharing photos of his toothless kids. He always carried a smile and had a positive attitude, even when things weren't going well. His uniform was usually squared away, and he rarely got upset about anything. Everyone liked Nick and looked up to him as an example of how to do it right.

We finally arrived at Baumholder in the middle of a winter storm. The airfield sat near a German forest with tall trees coated in white. I pictured good old Saint Nicholas flying overhead in a sleigh pulled by reindeer, but given the weather, nothing was airborne that day. The United States Army Garrison (USAG) Baumholder is nestled in the wooded hills of the Western Palatinate in the Rheinland-Pfalz area of Germany. The base is near Kaiserslautern, which is about eighty miles southwest of Frankfurt and 300 miles northeast of Paris.

No one knows why, but Baumholder had earned the nickname of "Rock" many decades earlier. I wondered if it had to do with the base's medieval origins dating back to around 1156. Maybe the original occupants sat around on big boulders while telling stories about knights on white horses, who knows.

The German army had used the base to train troops during World War II. To clear the area, they had displaced over 4,000 families and decimated vast swaths of farmland. After the war, the French occupied the base but turned it over to the U.S. Army in 1951. The Second Armored Division rolled in a bunch of tanks and upgraded the facilities. By 2011, Baumholder housed some 40,000 military and civilian personnel, making it one of the largest bases in Europe. One unit included the 92nd Military Police Company. Our small team was scheduled to spend the next few weeks training with this group and learning how to keep from dying in a combat zone. I thought about how many times I had "died" during Security Forces training years earlier and realized that once I got to Afghanistan, practice would be over. One mistake there could be my last.

Some of our training took place in classrooms at an air base in Sembach with instructors pointing at whiteboards or clicking through presentations projected onto screens. The rooms were medium sized with four or five rows of desks where atop each sat a ruggedized notebook computer. Along with a handful of us from Lakenheath, the class contained a mix of ranks and duties from across Europe, including enlisted members and officers.

Our outdoor training took place near the Baumholder Air Base. With dense snow covering the ground, and the temperature dropping to less than twenty degrees Fahrenheit at night, we shivered near fires and curled up tight in our sleeping bags. During the day, when the weather warmed to a balmy twenty-five degrees, we conducted simulated patrols, convoys, and IED sweeps. Occasionally, we stayed in a rundown German barracks that appeared to have been built during World War II. When I glanced at the aging brick walls, I imagined German soldiers cleaning rifles and filling canteens while preparing to battle Americans and Brits at dawn.

They gave us no liberty during our training, so we spent most of our time socializing on the base in our dormitories. There was no club or bar for enlisted personnel, so we visited a small shop on base to get snacks and beer. We drank Guinness while smoking, joking, and talking about our training. We made fun of our instructors' idiosyncrasies, but we were glad they were teaching us how to stay safe in a combat zone. Now and then someone mentioned our upcoming deployments to Afghanistan, and the room fell silent.

The last week of our training was the most difficult. They reminded us that Security Forces personnel protected people, property, and perimeters and as such were considered the frontline defenders of the Air Force. In this capacity, we again reviewed our Combat Airman Skills Training related to an active shooter scenario. I shuddered when I thought of how many times I'd been "killed" by terrorists in previous training exercises.

In this more advanced phase of our training, we learned about an innovative program from the U.S. Air Forces Central Command called Check Six. The "Six" refers to frequently checking your "six," which is behind you in reference to the six o'clock position if you're standing atop a large clock, with your nose facing the twelve. It also stands for the math used to remember a process for staying alive.

They designed the program to help us remove our instinctual blinders and rethink our comfort zones; to refocus our attention on what's going on around us—including "behind our butts," as the instructor admonished. The Air Force adopted the Department of

Homeland Security's definition of an active shooter as being an individual actively engaged in killing or attempting to kill people in a confined and populated area, typically by using a firearm. Usually, the active shooter has a vague or non-existent motive, so there's no coordinated pattern when selecting victims. In other words, the guy's a seriously messed up asshole trying to randomly blow people away.

Our instructor explained that no matter how well trained we might be, if civilians are in the area, they will panic and run for cover or freeze with fright and become easy targets. The Check Six program offered classroom briefings, field training, and frequent drills to improve our muscle memory to implement a process that employs the formula $3+2+1 = 6$.

Using this approach gave us three primary options: escape, barricade, or fight back. Unfortunately, regardless of which option we implemented, there were only two possible outcomes: live or die. I recalled what it felt like to "die" during training and decided I preferred the "live" option. I also learned that we had only one shot—no pun intended—to get it right. That's where the $3+2+1$ comes from. Three options, two outcomes, one shot.

Despite what we see in movies, on average, active shooter scenarios last only ten minutes. This makes rapid and accurate decision-making imperative to avoid being killed or wounded. The instructors designed our training to instill a self-defense culture by mentally preparing us to react instantly to any act of violence perpetrated against our base or those under our care.

Using actual weapons loaded with blanks, in similar fashion to my earlier training, our instructors subjected us to rigorous, difficult, and deadly scenarios. We all died frequently until we started working better as a team and learned how to bypass our fear circuits and act without delay. We had to overcome our natural "freeze factor." One second could mean the difference between life and death within the typical ten-minute active shooter window.

The most difficult part of these exercises required us to overcome our natural instincts to prioritize protecting a single individual over defending our base. This may sound uncaring, but just the opposite is true. In most cases, our base may house dozens or hundreds of civilians and military personnel, as well as a cache of weapons. While it's nearly impossible to allow someone to be killed or injured, a Security Forces airman may face this gut-wrenching choice. If an active shooter or several terrorists are seeking to penetrate a base, they could kill many people and gain access to weapons they could later use to slaughter even more individuals. A "base," we were told, could be something as large as Baumholder or as small as an Air Force bus. Our training taught us how to make split-second decisions to first prevent a base attack from happening before taking action to protect a single bystander. This was no simple task. We had to stand our ground to defend against an intrusion that could lead to far more loss of life, sometimes at the cost of watching a civilian get shot.

One of our instructors helped us deal with this Check Six inevitability by stating that our most important mission is to defend our base and protect the civilians and airmen under our care. This requires making tough decisions within seconds and sometimes taking the fight to the enemy.

That last sentence touched a chord. I recalled again the flames billowing from the sides of the Twin Towers, and from deep within my soul, a question formed. In an attack on a base or active shooter scenario, would I be willing to take the fight to the enemy?

Conviction welled up inside my chest, and I knew the answer was a resounding yes.

We completed our training in late January 2011, boarded our bus, and returned to Lakenheath. I then went from one icy freezer to another.

CHAPTER 11:

PUZZLE PIECES

Icy cold rain and snow sludge covered the ground in England, and I brought it with me to New Jersey. When I stepped off the plane at the Newark Airport, I was surprised to see the smiling face of my former boss, Edward Barber, who was now an E-7 master sergeant. He was also attending the same intel school, heard I was flying in, and gave me a ride to the base. We reminisced about our time in Portugal and swapped stories about our duty stations and travel since then. Edward was now stationed at Nellis Air Force Base near Las Vegas, Nevada, and by chance had also been selected for the January Force Protection Intelligence training course. He wasn't deploying to Afghanistan, at least not yet, but after completing this course, his name would certainly be thrown into the hat. Given that he was married and had kids, he wasn't excited about potentially going to a war zone someday.

Fort Dix is a joint base, operated by the U.S. Army, Navy, and Air Force. It's about sixteen miles southeast of Trenton, New Jersey, and had been built during World War I. They had named the base after General John Adams Dix, who was a veteran of the War of 1812 and the Civil War. He later became a U.S. senator, secretary of the treasury, and governor of New York. Apparently, the guy got around.

Fort Dix had primarily served as an Army training facility, with rapid expansion occurring during the Vietnam War. They constructed a mock Vietnamese village on the base to train soldiers prior to deployment. Since that time, Fort Dix has served as a preparatory training facility for military personnel serving in Bosnia, Iraq, and Afghanistan. On the flip side of that coin, there's also a Fort Dix Federal Correctional Institution (FCI) nearby where over 4,000 federal and military criminals wear orange jump suits and eat lunch off metal trays. On our way to the base, Edward joked that if I failed the training program, I'd be sent to the FCI. I didn't laugh.

As we drove down the New Jersey turnpike, with our windshield under attack by a snowstorm, Edward explained that the Air Force had taken over part of the base in 1987. At that time, Fort Dix had been on a closure list until the U.S. Air Force Security Police Air Base Ground Defense school moved there from Camp Bullis, Texas. That proved ineffective, so they moved back. Somehow, the base avoided a shutdown, and after 9/11, became a mobilization point for reserve and National Guard troops, as well as a home for the intelligence course we were about to complete at the Expeditionary Center. Edward said others he knew who had completed the course were impressed with the instructors and curriculum. The 421st Combat Training Squadron had apparently assembled a diverse group of instructors with extensive force protection and field combat experience. They had excellent facilities, equipment, and training materials, and those who graduated usually became some of the best intelligence analysts in the military.

Terrorist factions obviously had realized this and tried to strike a blow at the heart of one of the infidel's most important anti-terrorist training centers. On May 8, 2007, six terrorists, mostly ethnic Albanian Muslims, were arrested for plotting an attack against Fort Dix. The Islamic radicals were inspired by Taliban and al-Qaeda ideologies and planned to storm the base while brandishing automatic weapons. Their aim was to kill as many of the base personnel, students, and instructors as possible before either being killed or taking their own lives. Fortunately, law enforcement agents prevented the attack, but ever since that day, Fort Dix had remained on an uneasy high-alert status.

Edward and I survived our trek to the base without being attacked or skidding off an icy road. Exhausted from my flight from the UK, I found my bunk in the barracks and crashed for the night. The next morning, early but not bright, I met Edward at the door to our classroom. Clutching a cup of strong military coffee, I took a seat and waited for our instructor to arrive. Just before the class started, an Air Force airman rushed through the door and slid into a seat next to me. She was a petite woman with black hair and riveting brown eyes. She glanced over and smiled. My heart fluttered. I'd been so busy training and prepping for my upcoming excursion into a battle zone that I'd not had time to even consider a romantic relationship. I'd also not met anyone in the past year who'd made my heart skip and my throat tighten. She smiled and introduced herself as Rachel, and it was all I could do to keep my mind...and my eyes...on the instructor as he strode through the door.

A tall and erect first lieutenant in a crisp, blue uniform walked toward the podium. He had short, brown hair and a tight mustache. He motioned for us to sit and introduced himself as Victor Sanders, the course director for the 421st Combat Training Squadron. During our three-week course, he and others on his team would do their best to mold us into Air Force Intelligence experts. Until now, I had thought of myself as a base cop. When I'd enlisted, I'd never envisioned becoming an intel guy. Thoughts of Jack Ryan, the main character in Tom Clancy novels, popped into my head. Ryan was an analyst frequently thrust into the role of a field operative. While we really weren't analysts, and I didn't expect to be saving the world from annihilation while riding aboard a Russian nuclear submarine as Ryan had done in *The Hunt for Red October*, I learned that I'd be trained to provide intel support for combat forces in Afghanistan. If I messed up, the lives of our troops could be at stake. Despite being jet lagged, I did my best to stay alert and listen.

Our intel class had a few dozen students from various Air Force commands. We were told that many of us might wind up working together in the field—especially if we were bound for Afghanistan— as part of a joint coalition effort. In our first briefing, they gave us an overview of all the typical intel terms—although most of us already knew them. Our jobs would entail collecting and analyzing intelligence information from several sources, including various signals and communication mediums such as radio, satellite, cell phone, radar, etc. They called this SIGINT for signals intelligence. Human intelligence, or HUMINT, consisted of information collected from informants or overhearing conversations in a local market. These tidbits were like small puzzle pieces, each one by themselves indecipherable, but as a whole they could form important pictures about what the enemy was planning or doing.

Lt. Sanders told us about the German Oberursel during World War II. This was a special Luftwaffe German Air Force Intelligence unit that had been masterful at extracting minor details from captured Allied pilots and crews. While the POWs didn't think they were giving the Germans any useful information, each small morsel became an important piece of a larger puzzle.

The Oberursel intelligence team collected data from a variety of sources, including POWs, and filtered it up to the Luftwaffe's air defense commands. A typical conversation between a captured Allied pilot and a German interrogator might start casually, perhaps during an elegant dinner where prisoners were treated to fine food and wine. Speaking fluent English, the interrogators might talk about a German mission that was canceled because too many pilots had head colds and could not handle the high altitude. The Allied pilot, not believing that he was offering anything useful, might let slip that he'd once been grounded before a mission that was above 10,000 feet, where pilots needed to use oxygen masks. The Germans now had an important piece of intel about Allied mission parameters.

A German pilot at the dinner table might relate an interesting story about a recent mission he'd flown, offering details about his home airfield, course headings, and mission objectives. He'd then encourage an American P-47 fighter pilot to tell his side of the story, thus revealing the departure location, how high he had climbed, and when he had dropped depleted fuel tanks near the Dutch border.

The German pilot might say that a fighter group had reported the American pilots coming from the northeast, and because of a height advantage, had shot down several German Fw 190 aircraft before the Me 109s could arrive. The Allied pilot might then confirm the details, again providing important strategic information. This type of conversation might last an hour during dinner while scribes in a back room jotted down the details. The German Oberursel interrogators rarely asked specific questions, certainly nothing that might spook a pilot, but learned important P-47 flight details including altitudes, fuel ranges before dropping tanks, fighter tactics, and more. The

Luftwaffe's home defense command now knew when P-47 escorts might be forced to turn back and leave Allied bombers unescorted, or turn over these duties to longer-range P-51 or P-38 fighters. During this window of time, especially if the new escorts were delayed, the bombers were more vulnerable to attack.

The Germans bolstered their intel collection by combing through the remains of shot down Allied aircraft. Many airmen, and especially Americans, were not well trained in operational security. They frequently violated regulations and brought aboard unit photos, scribbled notes, personal letters, and sometimes even copies of operational orders. Some of these items survived plane crashes and were recovered by Oberursel analysts. The Luftwaffe intelligence unit also got copies of U.S. Army and British newspapers through neutral embassies. The *Stars and Stripes* paper often contained photos and information about American air units and their operations.

Analysts matched intel gathered from wreckage sites against Luftwaffe fighter and flak unit records to determine how the bombers had been shot down. They obtained additional information during prisoner interrogations and matched that against debris taken from downed aircraft. Luftwaffe signals intelligence units, consisting mostly of young women who spoke fluent English, also eavesdropped on radio chatter between Allied aircraft and ground stations. By late 1943, using a treasure trove of photographic intelligence (PHOTINT), HUMINT, and SIGINT, the Germans could determine an accurate order of battle for American and British air forces—including call signs, mission objectives, and unit stations. This offered an array of tactical intelligence that helped the Luftwaffe shoot down thousands of American and British bombers and fighters flying missions over Europe.

After World War II, the Soviets copied many of the German tactics and also became masters at the intel collection game. When the Cold War escalated, U.S. military units stepped up their intelligence-gathering capabilities to counter the new threat.

While sitting in the Air Force intel class and listening to my instructor talk about how this art had improved over the years, I squirmed in my seat. I realized that dozens of lives might one day depend on how well we learned our trade and did our jobs in the field. I grabbed another cup of coffee, fought off my fatigue, and cocked an ear.

Sanders explained that we needed to become proficient enough to not just gather the intel and analyze it, but also to suggest strategies and tactics to counter enemy threats. We needed to predict their chess moves on the game board and recommend countermoves. The end goal was to create an intelligence brief that offered a clearer picture of what was happening on the ground so officers in the field could make informed battle and deployment decisions.

During our break, Rachel and I sipped coffee, ate stale pastries, and made small talk. She had flown in from Aviano Air Base, where I'd spent two years before being transferred to Lakenheath. Like me, she had become enthralled with the European sights in and around Italy, and of course, with the amazing pizza. She blushed when I said that it didn't appear she'd consumed much of it. She countered by saying that she most definitely had, which had forced her to double up on morning runs.

The break ended, and I reluctantly returned to my seat wearing a grin from ear to ear. Our instructor glanced over at me and Rachel and flashed us a puzzled look as we appeared to be the only ones in the room enjoying the class. When the day finally ended, I invited Rachel to dinner. Given the weather conditions, which meant placing our mess hall trays next to each other while sipping orange juice from a carton. I didn't care. Perhaps for the first time in my Air Force career, I actually enjoyed the military cuisine.

Walking outside in the freezing weather while holding hands was not in the cards, so we stayed up later than prudent in a lounge area while talking nonstop. Conversation was easy and natural. We became instant best friends while crunching on chips and watching movies in her barracks room. Over the next few days, our friendship blossomed into something more, but there was always an uneasy tension. Neither of us wanted to think or talk about the inevitable. We were both heading to Afghanistan, but I was going to Kandahar and she to Bagram. I cursed the bad luck, but nothing short of a divine miracle could alter our destinies. We decided to simply enjoy the short time we had together and let the future unfold as it may.

During our first week in class, they gave us a detailed overview of typical intelligence scenarios, which included integrated base defense, the proper use of surveillance reconnaissance assets, and dealing with asymmetric threats. We also learned how to use proper intelligence techniques to prepare troops for various mission deployments. Several students in the class raised hands to ask questions. One tech sergeant from the 93rd Bomb Squadron at the Barksdale Air Base in Louisiana asked about the importance of communications between different units and especially between different branches, such as the Army, Navy, and Air Force.

Sanders told us that Air Force HQ had previously determined a need to train intelligence personnel to support field combat operations and force protection, so we could assume various intel roles in Iraq and Afghanistan. Interbranch communications had been a problem, which is why several days in class were now devoted to learning about the roles of various counterparts in other branches and operational functions, so we could combine intel and create a complete picture. This approach had proven vital to success, as intelligence analysts conducted aircrew pre-mission briefings and debriefings, analyzed attack trends and surface-to-air threats, and briefed senior officers on tactical and strategic security threats in their area of operations.

The course designers packed a lot of information into a small window. In the first week, we learned how to view our operational environment from the perspective of operators across several military branches who were "outside the wire" of our security perimeter. Also, we learned how to tailor the intel we collected to their specific needs—as well as their need to know. There would be times when we could not share all the details because of classification levels.

As the class progressed, I gained a better understanding of various enemy capabilities, threats, equipment, and tactics, and how to counter these and prepare our troops prior to deployment. Even though we were Air Force, and focused mostly on air threats, they also showed us how to cooperate with other branches to support ground troops.

I met one student, a sergeant from the 204th Intelligence Squadron at McGuire Air Force Base in New Jersey, who was also deploying to Afghanistan. When he spoke about his upcoming deployment, I could tell he felt the same way I did: both excited and nervous about serving in a combat zone. I wasn't overly concerned about my own life, as I'd be operating mostly inside security perimeters, but I was worried about ensuring the safety of others. One wrong intelligence conclusion or briefing mistake could prove fatal.

During the second week, I thought my brain was going to explode. While I could easily answer questions related to the range of surface-to-air missiles, I was not as knowledgeable about mortar round ranges or how IEDs were constructed, placed, and hidden from view in Afghanistan. Given that our pilots and aircrew were in greater danger of death or injury from these weapons, it was vital that intel analysts memorize details about any and all threats to military personnel in the field. In the last week, after a battery of written tests, the course concluded with a three-day, real-world scenario that included a grueling field training exercise designed to reinforce what we'd learned. We used real-time intel coming out of Afghanistan and other war zones to create presentations, analyses, and recommendations, as if we were actually preparing briefs for field commanders or troops deploying on convoys or missions.

When we had completed our last day of training in New Jersey, as Edward's rental car idled and sent a plume of exhaust smoke into the chilled air, Rachel and I ducked behind a building to say goodbye. We kissed and held each other tight. Rachel's lip quivered as tears filled her eyes. We promised to stay in touch, text often, and meet again the next time we both had leave.

With heavy feet and a heavy heart, I left New Jersey and flew back to England feeling prepared and ready to deploy to Kandahar Airfield to help keep operators safe from terrorist attacks. I had no way of knowing that my fellow airmen and I would come under fire from a terrorist attack long before we ever made it to Afghanistan.

In late February 2011, with only about a week remaining before I deployed to Afghanistan, sleeping soundly was not easy. Excitement and fear about what lay ahead kept me tossing and turning in my bed. Snow plastered windshields in the UK and coated roads in frosty white. I spent a few hurried days gathering the gear I'd need in Afghanistan and getting my personal house in order. I had to get vaccination shots, medical exams, and final briefings. I also had to write the most difficult letters of my life.

In case I did not come back from this assignment, I wrote a final goodbye letter to my parents. My hand shook while doing so. I thanked them for my childhood years and the love they had given me, for helping me to learn right from wrong and encouraging me to serve my country, and for being the kind of parents I could be proud of and love unconditionally. I had always felt pretty lucky to have been born under their roof, and in my final letter—which I hoped they would never read—I wanted to let them know how I felt.

I also wrote a letter to Rachel. Although we hadn't had enough time in New Jersey to go beyond the start of a romantic relationship, in the event anything happened to me in Afghanistan, I wanted to let her know how I felt. I also sent her an email wishing her the best on her journey to Bagram. She replied with the same wishes for me.

During my last week at Lakenheath, I spent time with several of the other airmen who were also deploying to Afghanistan. We'd all be flying together to Frankfurt, where we'd spend a few layover days at Ramstein before boarding a military transport plane bound for Kandahar.

Nicholas Locke had dark brown hair, stood over six feet tall, and had the chiseled jaw of a comic book hero. Women melted whenever he walked past, but he'd already given his heart to a blond-haired, blue-eyed beauty from England. Nicholas liked to spend hours in the gym and on the golf course. I also enjoyed golfing, and although I didn't have nearly as good a handicap, Nicholas and I often talked about the latest tournaments.

Although Nicholas was a few years younger than most of us, he displayed a great deal of maturity and polish. He took pride in being squared away, performing his duties, and getting along with almost everyone. He rarely lost his cool and always lent a hand to those who were falling behind. This was his first deployment "in country" but you'd never know it. He remained calm and unfazed. His only regret about going was having to leave his wife behind for six months. He and Nick Alden commiserated about spending long months away from their families. Nick had previously served in Iraq where airmen had been killed or seriously wounded. He didn't talk about it much.

Staff Sergeant Kyle Ritter had recently turned twenty-six and was senior to me even though we were the same rank. He'd oversee our band of fourteen during our trip, and I'd be his second. Not that it mattered much, as we'd only be together for a few days in transit. Kyle's bright blue eyes and jovial face helped lighten up any room. He wore thick, black-rimmed glasses that made him look like a book nerd, which seemed appropriate given his sharp mind and mathematical prowess. He could instantly calculate almost anything in his head. Kyle had grown up in the rural coal mining community of Irwin, Pennsylvania, and loved nature, being in the wild, and hunting. He lived there with his wife, his stepson, and their daughter—who had just turned two. Kyle talked about his family non-stop and often said he was dreading the thought of being separated from them for six long months.

Two other airmen, Madison Lane and Brad Winters, were less enthusiastic, but they squeaked out smiles now and then and were ready to do their duty and serve wherever they were sent. Madison was a petite blond with a sparkling personality. Brad was average height with brown hair and eyes, and although he wasn't married, he'd grown fond of life in England and did not want to trade a warm pub with fish and chips for a cold barracks with powdered eggs.

Despite their situation or the required sacrifices, everyone was willing and prepared to face whatever dangers lay ahead. At least, that's what we thought before we boarded our flight to Frankfurt.

CHAPTER 12:

THE TERROR

On March 1, 2011, I felt like someone had thrown me into a blender and turned it on high. There were a million last-minute details that needed tending to, including paperwork, packing, prepping, and people pleasing. The latter was necessary to encourage some individuals to help me complete a few tasks, or at the very least, not shuffle my stuff to the bottom of a stack. Sometimes I offered doughnuts, candy, beer, Scotch, cigars, or whatever it took to illicit a smile and a nod. The military, like many large organizations, revolves around personalities. Most are helpful and pleasant, a few aren't, but nearly all are busy and just trying to do their jobs. It helps to thank them for their hard work, give them a sincere compliment, and maybe a gift...like a Snickers bar.

Exhausted, excited, and nervous, I drove home. I spent the first part of the evening buttoning up my Beck Row home for a six-month sabbatical. I loved it there and had decided to keep the place during my deployment as it would be difficult to find another rental when I returned. Brad and Sarah had agreed to watch it for me, and that evening they treated me to a home-cooked meal before my deployment.

Brad had previously served in Afghanistan and did his best to tamper my anxiety by reminding me I'd spend most of my time inside a fortified compound. Still, I had heard stories about mortars and rockets being lobbed over fences, or terrorists trying to drive bomb-laden trucks through checkpoints.

That night, after dinner with Brad and Sarah, I glanced up at a blanket of bright stars while strolling home. I wondered what those stars might look like from Afghanistan. I wondered if Rachel, who had already deployed, was also gazing at those stars from Bagram. And I wondered if an angry terrorist was staring at that same night sky while contemplating how he was going to kill me.

The alarm jolted me out of bed at 5 a.m. on March 2. I yawned, stretched, and completed my morning routine. Strangely, I did not feel any angst or worry about deploying. I felt at peace and resigned to whatever dangers lay ahead. I zipped up my two military camouflaged rolling bags, grabbed my backpack, and walked out into the frosty morning air. Brad stepped outside about the same time, as he was heading into Lakenheath to start his day. His breath misted as he again tried to assuage my fears about flying into a war zone. I assured him I was fine while throwing my bags into the trunk of my car. I handed him a spare set of keys, and he promised to check on my car and fire up the engine now and then. I drove onto the base and parked in a long-term area near one of the barracks.

Tired from lack of sleep, I met up with the other thirteen airmen on our team at one of the Lakenheath dormitories. I found a steaming pot of black coffee on a table and poured a cup. We spent the next hour talking about our respective deployments and exchanging light banter. Someone said I looked like one of the scruffy street dogs we'd probably see in Afghanistan. Someone else said I looked more like a wild wolf who'd stayed up all night to howl at the moon. I slammed my hand against an uncooperative vending machine and said I felt more like a hungry Taco Bell chihuahua. Nick walked over and helped me with the machine while wishing Kevin a happy birthday. He had just turned twenty-two. Someone slapped Kevin on the back and said he'd finally have to start acting like an adult. We all shared a laugh before double checking our gear and trying not to think about where we were headed.

Following protocol, our deployment manager had instructed us to wear civilian clothing to avoid being noticed by terrorists as military personnel. Given that we'd all be wheeling camo duffle bags and locked rifle cases, we didn't think our blue jeans and sneakers would fool anyone. When not standing next to our bags, if our buzz cuts didn't give us away, our American accents and frequent military jargon would. You can take the airman away from the base, but you can't take the base away from the airman.

Later that morning, in front of the Security Forces dormitories, family members and fellow squadron members bid us farewell. Our deployment manager then gave us a final briefing before we departed. He again cautioned us not to stand out to avoid being spotted by bad guys. Most of us just shrugged. We were more focused on the potential dangers awaiting us in Afghanistan. None of us imagined that we'd come under fire in Frankfurt.

The fourteen of us stood, stretched, and clambered onto the Air Force bus bound for Heathrow Airport. We checked in at the British Airways counter and then sat around for another hour until our flight boarded. It was nearly impossible to seat all of us together, so we were scattered about the plane. I closed my eyes and dozed off shortly after the exit doors closed, and I believe most everyone else did as well.

My nap was short, as the flight only lasted about ninety minutes. When the airplane's tires screeched on the tarmac, I opened my eyes, yawned, and grabbed my backpack. The fourteen of us, trying not to act too "airman," strolled through the long and winding corridors in Terminal Two at Frankfurt Airport. The area was bright, polished, and smelled like floor wax. Around me, I heard a cacophony of voices speaking a myriad of different languages from across Europe.

A German business executive kept saying *hallo* and *bitte*. An Italian family, obviously excited about being on vacation, often uttered *prego* and *per favore*. An elegant woman, likely from Spain, kept saying *tener cuidado* to a porter who couldn't stop smacking her bags against trash cans and pillars.

We rode up and down escalators until we reached the baggage claim area. We collected our camo bags and then walked over to the special baggage area to grab our locked weapons containers. It took forever to sort out which belonged to whom, and when finally done, we exited the secured area and entered the main terminal. Nicholas Locke said he'd walk outside to hunt down our bus. Long minutes passed before he returned with a tall airman who was in uniform and introduced himself as Airman First Class Zachary Cuddeback from the 86th Vehicle Readiness Squadron at Ramstein Air Base. He'd drawn the duty that day to be our bus driver. He wore a permanent grin and said we were lucky. He motioned toward the sky beyond the large windows of the terminal and said the forecast for the day was bright and sunny with only a slight chance of boredom during our ride to Ramstein. Zachary then bent at the waist and motioned a hand toward the exit. He smiled and said our limo awaited us at curbside, complete with cushioned seats, bottles of champagne, and soft mellow jazz for our ride to the base. He also joked about not being important enough to warrant a police escort.

Zachary escorted us to the Air Force bus parked near the terminal. The long, blue-gray vehicle had a dozen windows and two rectangular air conditioning units on the roof—one forward and one aft. There was no storage area beneath the bus, so we hauled our stuff through the small open doorway and stowed everything in the first few seats. Gear and weapons were loaded onto seats in the front of the bus, so we all sat starting from the middle of the bus to the rear. Only Zachary Cuddeback remained near the front.

I sat on my hard bus seat and glanced out the window. The late afternoon sun splashed beams of yellow across the glass. The sunbeams undulated like ripples of water on a pond. I glanced over as Nick, after stowing his gear, said he was stepping outside to have a smoke. Even though I didn't smoke, I thought about joining him just to get a breath of fresh air before our ride, but I decided to remain inside.

Brad leaned over from across the aisle and asked if I was nervous. I shook my head and said I had been, but right now, I felt fine. I was resigned to whatever lay ahead. Now that we were one step closer to our destination, it didn't seem so concerning. I said that was probably due to our training. Nothing could be as bad as getting killed a dozen times by our instructors. Brad laughed and I got that right.

I heard a loud pop from outside the open bus doors and looked up but saw nothing. I swiveled my head and scanned the road beyond the windows. The noise had sounded like a car running over a rock, but I didn't see any passing vehicles. I looked at Brad, who was rifling through his backpack and didn't seem to have noticed. I glanced around the bus. No one else was cocking an ear or looking out a window. I shrugged and decided it was probably nothing. Then I felt the bus rock as someone climbed the stairs to enter and figured Nick must have finished his cigarette.

From the front of the bus, someone yelled, "Allahu Akbar!" I thought one of the guys was kidding around until I heard an ear-splitting boom. A surge of adrenaline shot through my veins. I sat up and saw red blood spraying from the side of Zachary's head as he slumped in the driver's seat. The sulfur smell of gunpowder filled the air. I moved my eyes right. A gaunt man in a gray hoodie stood in the aisle. A strand of black hair covered his forehead. His eyes were dark and filled with rage. His brow furled. He swiveled left and pointed a pistol at someone else, but I could not see who it was.

The assailant again screamed, "Allahu Akbar!" He fired his weapon four times in rapid succession. I recoiled and crouched down. I instinctively reached for my sidearm but felt nothing. I wasn't wearing one. My locked gun case was a few seats in front of me. My brain calculated the odds of reaching it, loading my rifle, and firing back. The answer came back in less than a second. I'd be dead long before I got off a shot. I grabbed the straps to my backpack and prepared to use it as my only weapon.

Still ducked down, I heard the shooter again yell "Allahu Akbar!" Two more deafening booms reverberated off the glass windows. Someone else screamed and then went silent. My heart pounded at breakneck speed. I prayed for a miracle but was certain I was seconds away from death. No amount of training had prepared me for this. I forced myself to stay in control while gripping my backpack straps even tighter. I wasn't going down without a fight.

The shouting and firing stopped. A strange silence filled the bus. Anger welled up inside me like a volcano about to blow. Memories from my Check Six training flashed into my brain. While still crouched, I briefly poked my head into the aisle. I glanced behind me. The rear door was closed. No additional assailants were attacking us from our "six." I then recalled the formula.

Three.

We had three options: escape, barricade, or fight back. I did not see a way to escape. If we tried to climb out a window or run for the back door, we'd be gunned down. We couldn't barricade. We weren't armed and all we had to hide behind were bus seats. That left fight back. But how? With a backpack?

Two.

There were only two possible outcomes. Live or die. I'd do whatever it took to ensure the former, for myself and my team.

The silence had lasted too long. Had the guy left?

One.

If the Tango was still on the bus, I had one shot to overcome my "freeze factor" and act.

I slowly inched my head above the seat. A pool of crimson coated the black rubber on the floor. My throat constricted. The gunman stood in the aisle a few feet away. He glared at me. He was young, in his early twenties. He barred his teeth and pointed the pistol at my forehead. I focused on the black hole inside the metal cylinder.

I wondered if it was the last thing I'd ever see.

The dark man screamed, "Allahu Akbar!"

He squeezed the trigger.

I flinched and blew out a breath.

Click.

Nothing exploded.

I could hardly breathe as my heart raced even faster.

"Allahu Akbar!"

Click.

Again, no boom.

I wondered if I was already dead—or if the gun had fired and deafened my hearing—or if I was in shock and about to die. My mind filled with images of my home, my parents, my siblings: the postcard snapshots of my life. The surreal moment lasted only a second and then evaporated.

The terrorist looked at his gun, growled, and turned to run. He bolted off the bus and disappeared. I sprang to my feet and slipped on a river of crimson streaming across the floor. My knee skidded across the pool of blood. I stood up and quickly assessed the situation. Zachary and Kevin were motionless.

Airmen on the bus sprang into action. Two attended to Kyle, who had been shot twice. One of the rounds had hit him in the head. He was bleeding profusely, and an airmen had to hold him down while others attended to his wounds.

I sprinted off the bus and found Nick lying on the ground. I quickly checked for a pulse. Nothing. I wanted to double over. I wanted to fall to my knees and weep, but I had to find the will to press forward. I had to catch the assailant. I had to protect our people. Right now, that included any other service personnel or innocent bystanders. Despite the apparent gun jam, I couldn't be sure the terrorist had completed his rampage. If possible, I needed to apprehend the guy. My training in New Jersey had taught me that gaining intel from one captured Tango could save lives. We needed to know if the shooter was acting alone or part of a coordinated attack. Was he with a terrorist cell, and if so, was a larger attack imminent?

I ran at full speed toward Terminal Two, dodging luggage-wielding passengers along the way. Near the entrance, I scanned the area but did not see a gray hoodie. I moved my head right, squinted, and searched in front of Terminal One. Nothing. Then something. A dark flash. The man in the hoodie jogged through an open door. I sprinted toward him while yelling for someone to stop him. I shot past several stunned passengers and ran into the terminal. I didn't see the terrorist. Fear gripped my throat.

Had I lost him?

I moved my head back and forth. Still nothing. Then, I glimpsed the dark man running up a flight of stairs toward a mezzanine. I shot after him and leaped up the stairs, two at a time. On my left, I noticed another shape following close behind: a tall man in blue jeans and a T-shirt. I wondered if he might be another terrorist. If they were working together, I could run into a trap.

At the top of the stairs, I saw the assailant run toward a McDonald's on the right. I pursued him, being careful not to allow the other man to approach from my six. The terrorist turned toward me and backed against a wall. Now blocked, he could go no further right. He looked to his left toward a USO center near the McDonald's. His right hand gripped a knife. My heart thudded as I struggled to catch my breath.

I sensed the other man jogging up the stairs behind me. I turned my head slightly left, careful to keep both men in sight. The terrorist opened his eyes wider to look at the other man. I did not see recognition on his face. Wielding a fixed blade knife, the shooter glared at me. Instead of hate, I now saw fear in the man's eyes. He obviously knew he had been caught and would soon be taken into custody. My pulse quickened as I looked at the knife and wondered if he might lunge at me and jab the blade deep into my gut.

By now a crowd had formed near the McDonald's. A sea of color filled my peripheral vision as people pointed and murmured. The shooter panned his eyes back and forth between me, the man who'd run up the stairs, and the dozen onlookers nearby. Concerned that he might hurt one of them, I stepped left to keep him pinned. Time slowed. An eternity passed in a matter of seconds. Someone shouted in the distance. A deep male voice speaking German. The man standing next to me translated and said it was the German Federal Police. He had an American accent and said the police were ordering us to raise our hands.

I let out a breath and lifted my arms. The man next to me did the same. The shooter blared Allahu Akbar and waved his knife back and forth. A half-dozen German police officers approached and pointed pistols at the man's chest. Speaking both German and English, they ordered him to drop the weapon. I saw the rage in the terrorist's eyes change to fear. He finally dropped the knife and fell to his knees. Two officers ran over and cuffed the guy while two others stepped closer to question me and the American. One officer pointed at my blood-stained knee.

I lowered my arms and gave a quick synopsis of what had happened while the American ensured a clear translation. He said his name was Lamar Conner. He was a U.S. Army veteran and worked as a ticket agent at the airport. He confirmed the latter part of my story to the German police, stating that he'd seen me chasing the assailant and ran after us. I said I needed to check on my guys back on the bus. One officer said he'd go with me, and another said he'd call paramedics to the scene.

While most of the German police officers dealt with the shooter, I ran back to the bus with one officer in tow. When I arrived, I saw Nick's body on the ground near the bus and forced myself to check again check for a pulse. I placed two fingers on his cold neck. Nothing. He was gone. In my mind, I saw his smiling face. I recalled the faces of his wife and children as they laughed and played in their backyard. I watched Nick grin and walk off the bus for the last time. I again heard the pop from outside the bus doors as the dark man ended Nick's life. I now hated myself for not going with him when he had left the bus. If I had, perhaps he'd still be alive. Or perhaps we'd both be dead. Either way, I would have to live the rest of my life tortured by gut-wrenching guilt.

I again wanted to cry out in agony as I stared at Nick's placid face, but I had to find the will to press on. While the German officer radioed instructions to others on the way, I raised my chin, rose to my feet, and climbed back on to the bus.

The river of blood on the floor had congealed into something resembling sticky red paint. Zachary lay motionless in the driver's seat. A hole in his head dripped blood. A few airmen tended to Kyle, who was still unconscious but alive. I asked for a status update on the injured Airmen. They were alive, but not by much. I prayed that an ambulance would show up in time. I pulled one of the airmen aside and asked for a detailed assessment. He said that Staff Sergeant Ritter had been shot twice, and while he was still breathing, he didn't look good. I felt sick but tried not to show it as I asked about Kevin. He had been shot four times. I was shocked that he had been wounded that many times and was still alive. Someone pointed toward a hole in a window near the driver's seat and said one rounds had glanced off a rib and shattered the glass. Zachary and Nick had each been shot once in the head. Both were dead.

I closed my eyes and again heard the dark man in the hoodie scream Allahu Akbar followed by several loud booms. I recoiled with each shot. Someone placed a hand on my shoulder and said I needed to report the incident to our command at Lakenheath. I opened my eyes and nodded. I wanted to stay with my team, but knew I had to step off the bus and make the call.

I nodded and tiptoed across the sea of crimson on the floor. I found my backpack and removed my mobile phone. I told everyone that help was on the way, and I was going to call our command.

I stepped off the bus and tapped the command line number on my phone.

I heard a ring followed by a male voice. "Unit Deployment, this is Tech Sergeant Boyd."

I cleared my throat and tried to keep my voice steady. "This is Staff Sergeant Brewer. I'm with the 48th Security Forces in transit at the Frankfurt Airport. We were just attacked by a shooter, possibly a terrorist. Two confirmed dead, Senior Airman Alden, and Airman First Class Cuddeback. Two seriously wounded, Senior Airman Ortiz and Staff Sergeant Ritter. I've contacted the German police and there's an ambulance on the way."

Silence, followed by a frantic reply asking me to repeat what I'd just said. I did, this time even slower. Boyd was obviously frazzled. I lowered my timbre and gave him explicit instructions on what to do and whom to inform about the incident. Boyd acknowledged and said he'd send help ASAP. I gave him my number and disconnected.

Blue lights flashed atop two ambulances as they pulled to a curb nearby. Police vehicles followed close behind. German Bundespolizei (BPOL) officers exited doors and surrounded the area. They used ribbons and sheets of white and red plastic to cordon off a rectangle around the bus. Dozens of curious onlookers came over, stood beyond the plastic barriers, and murmured while pointing. A few medical personnel in blue jumpsuits wheeled a gurney toward Nick. They asked me what had happened, and I gave them a detailed account. Two of them checked for a pulse before placing Nick's body on a stretcher. Four others boarded the bus to retrieve Zachary and to tend to the wounded.

A wave of nausea made me double over as I stared at the sheet-covered body of Nick. Red blood had created a circle on the white cotton covering his face. Medical personnel arrived and wheeled off

Kevin and Kyle. I sucked in a breath and fought to maintain my composure. With Staff Sergeant Ritter wounded, the team needed me to step up and lead.

I checked on each member of the team, one at a time, to make sure no one else had been wounded or hurt. Everyone was shocked, distraught, and angry, but there were no other injuries. A German officer approached. He was a stocky man of medium height with a bent fighter's nose. A strand of blond hair poked out from the side of his uniform hat. In German-accented English, he asked if I was in command. I said yes, as our previous unit leader had been wounded. He nodded and said his officers would watch our bags while we were being interrogated.

I raised an eyebrow. "Interrogated?"

"Yes," the officer said. "You must all come with us now to be questioned."

CHAPTER 13:

THE AFTERMATH

The bodies of Nick Alden and Zachary Cuddeback remained at the scene as part of the criminal investigation conducted by the German police while an ambulance lit off its siren and screamed from the curb. Inside that vehicle, Staff Sergeant Kyle Ritter and Senior Airman Kevin Ortiz clung to a flicker of life.

I took a quick moment to send a text to my sister Tiffany to let her know I was okay and to pray for us. There were now eleven of us still standing. In military terms, that represented a 27 percent attrition rate, which is considered extremely dismal. Although we all wanted to accompany Kyle and Kevin to the hospital, the police required us to remain at the airport and accompany them to a private security area inside one terminal. Exhausted and distraught, we walked past curious onlookers and entered the building. Once inside, an officer delivered several bags of hamburgers and fries and handed them to us.

The airport police escorted us to a private holding area filled with cushioned airport seats. An officer tapped my shoulder and pointed toward a hallway. I lowered my head as I thought of Kyle and Kevin, and I prayed they were still alive. A tall German officer, in fluent English, asked me to describe what had happened starting from the time we had landed in Frankfurt. I was nervous but relied on my training to stay calm and deliver the details. When I got to the part where I had kneeled to check Nick's pulse, I couldn't keep from choking up. The officer seemed sympathetic and asked me to take my time. When I finished, the officer said he was sorry for having to ask so many questions and pointed toward the waiting area.

I stepped from the hallway and noticed a television mounted to a wall. The screen displayed images of our Air Force bus at the Frankfurt Airport, now surrounded by plastic barriers and ribbons of tape. Blue police car lights flashed as commentators thrust microphones toward the faces of various officers. While I could not see the bus through the airport windows, I knew it was not far away. I closed my eyes and shuddered as I recalled slipping on the blood running across the floor.

The buzzing of my phone made me jump. I glanced at the screen and saw that my parents were calling. It was now nighttime in Germany, which meant it was midday in the U.S. My mom's voice quavered as she asked if I was okay. I assured her I was fine. She asked a million questions, and I did my best to answer without providing any gruesome details. She handed the phone to my dad, who said he was proud of me and knew how I felt. He'd lost friends in Nam, and while I had sympathized with what he must have gone through, I had never really understood—not until now.

I promised to keep my parents informed and ended the call. I tapped out a quick text to my sister, Tiffany, to let her know I was okay. I then sent a text to Rachel, in case she was also watching the news, and then turned my attention to the television screen as an announcer delivered information about what had happened. My ears perked as the media updated a few details not long after we'd imparted that information to the police. I glanced around the room. There were a dozen airport police officers and several other individuals in civilian clothes. I had at first assumed the civilians were airport personnel, but now wondered if some media "spies" had slipped in as well. Either that, or someone was leaking information to the press.

None of us spoke much while we sat in the lounge and watched the news. A few hours passed before a senior master sergeant from Ramstein Air Base strode into the waiting area. He was a short man in his thirties with a tight mustache. He found me in a corner and said he was the base operations superintendent. He asked dozens of questions and nodded as I repeated what I'd told the police. The senior master sergeant then reached into his pocket and retrieved a coin. He held out his hand to shake mine, with the coin face up in his palm. I recognized the symbol printed on the coin as the Air Force Security Forces emblem. He was handing me a "challenge coin," a gesture indicating mutual respect and honor. My eyes teared up as I shook his hand and pocketed the coin.

The senior master sergeant said he was sorry that our team had to go through all of this, but it was unfortunately not going to be over soon. He said we now had to endure another several hours of interrogations at the Bundespolizei (German Federal Police) headquarters in Frankfurt. I groaned and shook my head.

A horde of passengers pointed and murmured while the airport police escorted the eleven of us to an area near our bus. The authorities had brought in a tow truck and hoisted up the bus at the front end to haul it somewhere. A dozen police officers gripped machine guns and formed a circle around the vehicle while scanning the crowd for bad guys. At first I thought they were going to let us retrieve our bags before driving us by police cars to the station. Instead, they asked us to board another bus that had just arrived.

The bus was cold, silent, and felt like a mortuary. My stomach churned as my shoes squeaked on the rubber floor. I found my seat and closed my eyes. The bus rocked and groaned as the rest of the team came aboard. Each time the vehicle shook, I recalled the angry eyes of the dark intruder and grimaced.

Thirty minutes later, we pulled away at a slow clip. I craned my head to examine the faces of the team. They were blanched and their jaws were tight. I knew they were fatigued and suffering from battle shock. They had briefed me about this in my training. Our instructors had warned us about what can happen to the brain after witnessing friends die on the battlefield. I'd been prepared for the eventuality and had expected something like this might occur in Afghanistan, but I'd never imagined a shell shock event happening to my team at a civilian airport in Germany.

The bus finally stopped in front of the Bundespolizei station in downtown Frankfurt. A million lights sparkled from nearby high-rise buildings as we stepped out into the frosty night air. Officers in crisp uniforms brought us into the building and confiscated everything we were carrying. They pointed toward restrooms and told us we needed to strip off our clothes and place them into evidence bags. They gave some of us random spare clothes that didn't fit right. I wondered if the police had confiscated them from drug dealers who were now doing time in German prisons, but I didn't ask. They didn't have enough hand-me-downs for everyone, so some airmen had to wear thin paper garments. I felt bad for my team. They had just watched four of our guys get blown away by a terrorist and had spent over three hours being interrogated by airport police and a New York counterterrorism unit. After all that, we were now being stripped of our clothes and treated like enemy prisoners. I knew the Bundespolizei were being as kind as possible and were only doing their jobs, but it didn't make it any easier.

One officer guided me into an interrogation room. Atop a single table in the middle sat a tape recorder. I sat in a folding chair and wiped my hands on the strange pair of pants that had probably been confiscated from a smuggler. I felt like I was the perp, and the police were about to drill me for three days until I confessed to a crime I didn't commit. Two detectives—a man and a woman—walked in and sat down. Both lit cigarettes. Pungent smoke filled my nose as the female detective switched on the recorder and asked me to state my name, rank, and unit information. The male detective introduced himself as Peter Klaus, Chief Investigator of the Federal Republic of Germany. He said they were all saddened by the loss of the two Americans and hoped that the other two would soon recover. He also said the German Republic was always grateful to America for its continued NATO support and for being a strong and enduring ally. I'm sure Klaus was being sincere, but at the time, it felt like a political speech for the recording. Klaus then asked me dozens of questions, most of which I'd already answered for the airport police.

When the interview concluded, three hours later, Klaus opened the door and motioned for me to leave. Another detective guided me to an area that held our valuables and helped me find my mobile phone and wallet. They kept the rest of my belongings. Several more hours passed while detectives questioned all of us and then finally allowed us to relax in a waiting room.

At one point we were all told that Kevin and Kyle were still alive, but in critical condition. We were all hoping for the best and praying for miracles. An officer approached and explained that we'd soon be escorted to Ramstein Air Base. Bleary-eyed and drained, we downed cups of coffee and folded our tired bodies into awaiting German taxi vans. Several police cars, with lights flashing, guided the vans out of the city and onto the road leading to Ramstein. Forty-five minutes later, we approached the gate to the air base. I glanced out the window and saw that the base had been locked down tight in a Force Protection Condition Delta. The guards at the gate were in their full battle rattle.

The vans pulled into a lot outside the base and let us out. Still wearing someone else's clothes or paper garments, we followed base personnel to the Deployment Transition Center on Ramstein. The large, hotel-like barracks was a counseling center and "halfway house" where the Air Force sent airmen returning from combat duty. The USO and Wounded Warrior Project gave us a fresh set of black sweatpants and sweatshirts to wear, and facility personnel gave us keys to separate rooms.

Although I'd never made it to Afghanistan, I felt like I had. I stood in front of the mirror in my tiny bathroom and gazed at my ashen cheeks and bloodshot eyes. I thought about Kevin, who'd likely suffered permanent damage, and Kyle, who was clinging to a dim hope in the hospital. I then thought about Zachary and Nick. Their cold, lifeless bodies were now lying on metal slabs in a Frankfurt morgue. I fell to my knees and sobbed until my tears ran dry, and then I finally forced myself to crawl into bed.

CHAPTER 14:

THE GENERAL

The next morning, after I'd tossed and turned all night, a bright sun beamed through the slats covering my window. Disoriented, I did not at first know where I was. Surreal and shocking images of the prior day flashed into my head. I was sure it had all been a nightmare, and once I splashed cold water on my face, the memories would fade along with the soap bubbles in the sink.

That didn't happen. I sat on the edge of my bed and relived each terrifying moment in slow motion: every Allahu Akbar, every thunderous boom, every drop of spilled blood.

Feeling like I'd gone fifteen rounds against a heavyweight champion, I pulled on my borrowed jeans and T-shirt and sauntered downstairs to grab a bite with my team. They were silent as they picked at their food. We said little and only occasionally locked sad eyes to share an unspoken understanding. We were the survivors and didn't want to be.

We learned that Senior Airman Kevin Ortiz, shot four times by the assailant, had miraculously lived. The doctors warned of permanent nerve damage to Kevin's arm. If true, he'd likely be forced to accept an early military discharge. If that happened, I knew it would break his heart.

Staff Sergeant Kyle Ritter had not fared as well. He'd been shot twice, once in the buttocks and once in the head. The first wound was relatively minor, but the second round had left him with survival very low chance of survival, according to the German doctors. He'd undergone five hours of trauma surgery, wherein they had removed over 30 percent of his skull and then placed him in a medically induced coma from which he might never awake. Even if he lived, they predicted a 90 percent likelihood of permanent brain damage. His wife had flown to Frankfurt to be by his side. We all prayed that Kyle would recover but knew the odds were dismal.

That afternoon, two tall men with buzz cuts and tight-fitting suits asked me to meet with them in small room to again explain what had happened. They displayed stern faces and struck me as either ex-military or government trained. I was right. One of them said they were with a special counterterrorism unit attached to the New York Police Department. Both were military veterans.

They told me that the perpetrator was a twenty-one-year-old man named Arid Uka. He was Muslim, but from Kosovo. Terrorist factions had apparently radicalized him, and the agents were trying to get Uka extradited to the U.S. to stand trial. Any information I could give them could help their case. I again explained what had happened in great detail while they asked dozens of clarifying questions. The two agents were cooperative but also competitive as they tried to one-up each other with clever interrogatives. An hour ticked by in slow agony before they finally ran out of questions. An agent opened the door and motioned for me to leave.

An hour later, I was cordially compelled to meet with two FBI agents. They looked a lot like the two NYPD agents. They invited me into another small meeting room with no windows and motioned toward a metal chair. One agent asked if I knew anything about the arrest of Hassan Nasr in 2003 and his subsequent interrogation at the Aviano Air Base in Italy. I said I'd been stationed at Aviano and had heard about the incident but knew very little. It had happened years before I enlisted. Another agent asked if I'd heard the name Ansar al-Islam. I thought for a moment and then said I recalled that, back in 2003, the CIA had uncovered evidence of Nasr's connections with this known terrorist group. The two agents looked at each other and then back at me. One explained that Ansar al-Islam terrorists might have also been in contact with Arid Uka and may have used the Nasr incident and subsequent non-extraditions of the CIA agents involved to help subvert the young man. I shook my head. Apparently, my premonitions about possible repercussions stemming from that incident had come true.

Later that evening, our team gathered in a lounge area to watch the news. On CNN, President Barack Obama offered his comments about the shooting. "I'm saddened and I'm outraged by this attack," Obama said from a podium. "I want everybody to understand that we will spare no effort in learning how this outrageous act took place."

"We don't have all the information yet," Obama continued, "and you will be fully briefed when we get more information, but this is a stark reminder of the extraordinary sacrifices that our men and women in uniform are making all around the world to keep us safe, and the dangers that they face all around the globe."

German Chancellor Angela Merkel added her opinion by saying, "There was an incident today where two American soldiers were killed at Frankfurt Airport. We don't know the details, but I would like to say how upset I am."

She expressed her condolences to the families and said Germany will "do everything we can to try and find out quickly what happened."

Philip Murphy, the U.S. ambassador to Germany, said he was "grateful for the assistance provided by German government officials in protecting U.S. servicemen and women, and in investigating this terrible act. In difficult times, Germans and Americans support each other."

Boris Rhein, the top security official in the German state of Hesse, said Arid Uka had apparently acted alone and there were no indications of a coordinated terrorist attack. Whether or not on his own, we all knew that Uka had been radicalized by terrorist factions. The last time U.S. forces stationed in Germany had been attacked was in 1986, during the bombing of a disco frequented by U.S. military personnel. Two soldiers and one civilian had been killed, and 230 others injured. A Berlin court later determined that Libyan leader Muammar Gaddafi had ordered the bombing.

In Uka's case, the shooting hadn't been ordered as much as inspired by a preacher and a movie. Uka's family were ethnic Albanian and had immigrated from Kosovo over forty years earlier. Although Muslim, they denied any hatred toward America or its allies. However, the twenty-one-year-old Uka had been born in the northern town of Mitrovica, which made him a Kosovo citizen. They had then brought him to Germany, which I found odd. His parents had been living in Germany for almost two decades before Uka was born. Why did they choose to return to Kosovo for Uka's birth and then come back to Germany less than a year later? Was there a reason they did not want their son to be born a German citizen?

Uka had been educated in Germany and had secured a part-time job at the Frankfurt Airport in the postal center, which gave him the ability to monitor typical transportation tactics used by military personnel. After the shooting, Bundespolizei raided Uka's apartment and found over 1,500 jihadist files on his laptop and MP3 player. Some of these were texts written by Pierre Vogel, a German Islamic zealot who'd been accused of fomenting hate against the U.S. and NATO countries. They also discovered that several months before the attack, Uka had dropped out of school before receiving his diploma but didn't tell his family. He instead lied and told them he'd graduated. Those who knew Uka during his twenty years of life described him as polite, introverted, and shy. Over the past few months, however, the young Muslim had stopped associating with friends and family and had become reclusive and non-communicative. That's when he started clicking on websites that contained radical jihadist content and dressing in traditional Salafist clothing. He also learned how to speak more Arabic.

The Bundespolizei uncovered evidence that Uka had wanted to make the trek to Iraq or Afghanistan to join terrorists in their fight against the West but hadn't yet done so. He'd made contact via the internet with an imam preacher named Sheik Abdellatif from the Da'wa group, who taught at a Salafist mosque in Frankfurt. The mosque had been under surveillance by authorities as it was a primary meeting location for radical Islamists. As I'd learned from the agents at the German airport, Uka had apparently also been in contact with the known terrorist group Ansar al-Islam.

While most Muslim imams preached the true Islamic principles of peace and love, many did not. Interestingly, Uka's grandfather from Kosovo was an imam who may have become radicalized. Many Albanians had converted to the Islamic religion during the Ottoman period in the fourteenth century. In the twentieth century, the Albanian nation underwent several dramatic changes brought about by decades of state atheism followed by a removal of anti-religious restrictions that spurred an Islamic religious revival. Unfortunately, this time around, the tenets preached by its leaders were not as kind or tolerant as before. By 2011, almost 60 percent of the Albanian population had converted to the Islam religion, but many were being led by more radical imam preachers.

Uka had been born in Kosovo. He was therefore a citizen of that country and considered himself Albanian, not German. When he contacted imams who preached extremist ideals, perhaps like his grandfather, they preyed upon his ethnic background and used that to turn him toward hatred and revenge. Uka was an educated adult and made his own choices, but once someone starts down the path toward radicalization, it's difficult to pull back on the reins. One tactic used by Sheik Abdellatif, Ansar al-Islam terrorists, and others like them includes visual and auditory stimuli. They had apparently motivated Uka to watch a 2007 American movie called *Redacted* directed by Brian De Palma. Although fiction, the movie was shot using a documentary approach that made it seem real—as if depicting actual recorded events about the Iraqi Mahmudiyah massacre rather than a Hollywood fantasy.

One scene in the movie, which Uka watched on YouTube, showed U.S. soldiers raping Iraqi Muslim women. Enraged by this, Uka posted on various forums that he believed the incidents were real and that Americans had indeed raped Muslim women and gotten away with it. Deeply angered, he encouraged other Muslims to join their brothers in a global war against the U.S. and its allies.

That's when Uka made the fateful decision to steal a Browning 9mm handgun from one of his brothers and use it to kill American military personnel. The gun was old and had not been well maintained, which is likely why it had jammed during the shooting at the airport.

Had Uka's brother taken better care of his gun, I'd probably be dead.

A day after we learned about Uka and his motivations for killing us, either from the news or officers on the base who'd been briefed by the German police, we received some good news. Staff Sergeant Kyle Ritter had awakened from his coma. He had called for his wife, who had not left his side. At first, she had been terrified that the doctor's predictions might come true; that Kyle might have severe brain damage. Tears of joy streamed down her face when Kyle asked for a cheeseburger and fries. That's when Amanda knew her husband was still Kyle. She smiled, placed his palm on her abdomen, and said *they* needed him to get better.

That afternoon, Air Force personnel asked our team to meet for a briefing in the lounge area of the Ramstein facility where we were staying. All of us were nervous. We knew Kyle was alive, but they had only given us a few sparse details. We didn't know if there had been permanent damage, and if so, how bad it might be. We gathered in a large room downstairs and exchanged nervous banter while we waited. The smell of bacon drifted in from the nearby kitchen. We'd been told that a senior officer on the base would deliver our briefing, but we were surprised when General Mark Welsh strode into the room. We all popped to attention. The four-star general smiled and motioned for us to sit. Welsh stood about six feet tall, and his oval face framed a warm smile. His eyes conveyed genuine concern as he found an open chair and sat. Welsh had graduated from the U.S. Air Force Academy in Colorado Springs and now served as the commander of all U.S. Air Force operations in Europe. He was responsible for over 600,000 military personnel and had taken the time to visit with us for the next hour.

He spoke with a sympathetic voice when he expressed great sorrow about what had happened. He also pledged to improve Air Force security procedures to ensure it never happened again. He then delivered some bad news by informing us that medical personnel stationed at Ramstein, who were in contact with the German doctors tending to Staff Sergeant Ritter, said he'd been hit in the forehead above his right eye. The round had drilled a hole through his skull and exited his neck without causing major damage, but due to ruptures from shattered bone fragments, Ritter might lose some sight in his eye. He might also suffer bouts of pain and memory loss for the rest of his life. We were all glad Kyle had survived, but we were saddened and angered that one hostile man had caused so much permanent pain and suffering.

General Welsh seemed to sense our mood as he stood from his chair. He invited us to come to his house the following day to meet his family and enjoy some steaks and beer. We all rose from our seats, saluted, and then thanked him for taking the time to meet with us. I could tell that General Welsh wasn't doing all this for show. He seemed genuinely concerned about our welfare.

The following day, we met various military personnel at the center who facilitated conversations among the Point of Transition members. I felt undeserving of this attention, as I had never made it to Afghanistan. One member I spoke with explained that even though we had not been in combat, we had all experienced a situation that could trigger PTSD reactions. We'd witnessed the murder and serious wounding of our friends and colleagues. We'd come close to being killed ourselves. In my case, the shooter had pointed a gun at my head and pulled the trigger. Twice. There were bound to be residual effects, up to and including PTSD. When I returned to Lakenheath, I'd likely meet regularly with a psychologist on the base who could help me understand how I'd been affected and how best to deal with any symptoms. These might include nightmares, fearful reactions to loud noises, constant vigilance, and even extreme trepidation around airports. Given that I was in the Air Force, having the latter reaction would not be good.

That evening, two military vans pulled up in front of our facility. Wearing jeans and T-shirts, we piled in for a short drive to the other side of the base. Out the window, I spied several residences reserved for senior officers. Most were small, two-story wooden structures guarded by tall birch and spruce trees that swayed in a light breeze. The vans cruised up a long driveway and stopped at a gate. A uniformed airman approached, and our driver clicked down his window. He showed his ID and had us all display our military IDs as well. The guard checked each one carefully before he opened the gate and waved us in. My eyes opened wide at the sight of the general's home. The two-story brick and wooden home looked like a mansion, with what appeared to be over 4,000 square feet of living space.

General Welsh's wife, Betty, met us at the door with a beaming grin and eagerly welcomed us inside. Although Betty had some help, she kept an immaculate home adorned with pleasant and inviting decor. The entry and living room had a distinct military feel, combined with a soft and elegant touch. The wall paintings displayed pastel landscapes and rural countrysides in shades of green, blue, and burnt orange. Wooden fixtures, bookcases, and small decorations offered a turn-of-the-century feel, as if we'd stepped into the home of a Civil War general. One wall displayed an array of family photos alongside pictures of a younger-looking Welsh posed next to battle-field buddies.

The general met us in the kitchen. He and his teenage daughter were putting the finishing touches on the meal for the evening. The savory scent of steaming vegetables and baking potatoes made my mouth water. The general greeted us with a smile and held up a large platter of giant steaks. He asked if we liked rib eyes and all eleven of us nodded our agreement. Welsh invited us into the backyard, where we sipped on German beer and listened to the steaks sizzle on an open grill. I noticed Betty had two enlisted aids, who I assumed could also cook, but General Welsh insisted on tending to the steaks himself.

None of us talked about the incident, but I occasionally saw someone staring off into the distance. We all wanted our entire team to be there with us. Despite General Welsh's generosity, and the possibility that some of us might not have made it back, we all wished we'd wound up in Afghanistan instead of Welsh's backyard. The general spent time with each of us, asking about our homes and families and why we had joined the Air Force. He did not talk about the shooting but instead focused on getting to know each of us personally. The general seemed to understand our situation and did his best to make us feel relaxed and at home. I was sure he had lost airmen under his command in the field, as he seemed to know exactly what we were all feeling.

After dinner, we relaxed in the general's large living room and had a few more beers. Fireplace logs crackled and popped, and the scent of burning wood reminded me of the holidays back home. About an hour later, Welsh tapped me on the shoulder and asked me to stand up in front of the group. Nervous about being called out in front of the team, I stood and stepped toward the fireplace. The general reached into his pocket, removed a large coin, and held out his hand. Shocked, I accepted his handshake and the challenge coin. My eyes welled up as the general placed a warm hand on my shoulder.

Welsh's face turned serious as he said I now had a responsibility to my team. Even though we might go our separate ways, as we'd soon be returning to our respective commands and on to subsequent deployments, I needed to continue to set an example as a leader. He said he was proud of my actions at the airport. He said I did the right thing by first checking on everyone, issuing orders, and then pursuing the shooter to ensure he did not kill or wound others. This action showed courage, fortitude, and demonstrated the core leadership tenants of the Air Force. Welsh then turned toward the group and said he understood we were all hurting and concerned about our wounded colleagues, but it was important that we also be there for each other. We had to remain in touch and support one another through this time of healing.

I looked around the room at the faces of everyone on our team and was glad I wasn't the only one with watery eyes. When the evening concluded, we thanked the general and his family for their hospitality and climbed back into the Air Force vans. That night, I slept a little better, but I knew it would be a long time before the nightmares dissipated. I also knew I'd never be "the old Trevor" again. I had lost much of my innocence on 9/11, and on 3/2 the remaining rose color in the glasses through which I viewed the world disappeared forever.

CHAPTER 15:

THE HEALING

The day following our dinner with General Welsh was one of the most difficult in my life. They asked me to join my team on the flight line—out on the tarmac at the Ramstein Air Base—for a dignified transfer. This is a formal process conducted for U.S. military personnel who are killed in a theater of operation. It's not a ceremony, but rather a solemn delivery of the transfer cases—or temporary caskets—to the transport plane that will fly the remains to Mortuary Affairs Operations at Dover Air Force Base in Delaware. There, an Air Force medical examiner will make a positive ID before releasing the bodies to the families for burial.

Although the official dignified transfer for members of the family would take place at Dover, General Welsh had decided to also do a transfer at Ramstein for our team. I instructed everyone that since we were all still in civilian clothes, we needed to wear similar outfits, so we'd look like a team. I asked the women to wear their hair formally in tight buns and the guys to be clean shaven.

On the tarmac, we lined up next to a dozen other uniformed airmen from Ramstein. We'd all been given white gloves to wear. Nearby, a large cargo transport plane sat alone with the ramp open and waiting. The dense smell of aircraft fuel hung heavy in the chilled morning air. My heartbeat escalated as I scanned the flight line. The black silhouette of a hearse formed at the edge of the runway as it veered around the side of a building.

Others based at Ramstein lined the route to show their respects. Escorted by German police cars, the hearse rolled to a stop near the back of the plane. Airmen in dress uniforms opened car doors and stepped onto the tarmac. I heard a brief sob from someone to my right. A wave of nausea hit my gut as I looked through the back windows of the vehicle. Two dark caskets sat side by side. I knew one held the body of Airman First Class Zachary Cuddeback. Inside the other lay the remains of Senior Airman Nick Alden.

With all the self-control I could muster, I held my chin up and watched the base honor guard grab the casket handles. They marched as a carry team over to the cargo transport plane and place the caskets on the cargo loading equipment. We stood at attention and saluted. The engines whined as the plane lumbered down the runway and lifted off the ground.

Senior Airman Kevin Ortiz and Staff Sergeant Kyle Ritter remained in a German hospital in Frankfurt while the eleven of us who had not been physically wounded returned to Lakenheath in the UK. Our unit sent an escort for each team member and flew us back aboard a KC-135 refueler from the Mildenhall Air Base. Members of our unit greeted us at Mildenhall and ferried us to Lakenheath. In the dorm common areas, a congregation from our unit welcomed us home. While we were heartened by this, gone was any light banter or joking. Gone were any bright eyes or zeal for life's adventures. Gone was any hope for a normal or happy life, at least not any time soon.

They took most of us off the front line and placed us on desk jobs at Lakenheath. The Air Force, rightly so, didn't think we were quite ready to resume our security duties. My home in Beck Row was cold and silent, and even though I didn't feel like being social, I found myself on a stool at the Rose and Crown most evenings.

Colonel John Quintas, Lakenheath's base commander, scheduled a memorial service for Nick Alden and General Welsh flew in for the event. They asked me to say a few words on stage in Nick's honor. A few weeks later, a few of us were granted leave to fly to the United States to attend Nick's funeral.

The dawning of spring brought with it the rich scent of red cedar and sweet magnolia in the rural community of Anderson, South Carolina. Four of us on the team were met at the airport by a technical sergeant who drove us to a small motel in town. We didn't feel like going out that night, so we stayed inside and ordered room service. The next morning, wearing our dress uniforms, we met with Nick's family at a local church. When I saw Nick's children, my gut knotted and I could barely contain my grief.

About fifteen minutes before the service started, a black SUV rolled to a stop in front of the church. Uniformed airmen stepped from the vehicle and stood at attention. One opened a back door to allow Brigadier General Jimmy E. McMillian, the director of Security Forces, to exit the car. A tall and distinguished African American, McMillian placed an officer's cap adorned with gold leaves atop his salt and pepper hair. He wore a blue uniform decorated with a row of ribbons. Since 1982, McMillian had earned a stellar reputation while serving in a variety of Security Forces roles.

In keeping with Nick's religious upbringing, the funeral was a formal and spiritual affair. The women wore black dresses and the men black suits with ties. We sat on pews while a church leader delivered a speech, followed by speeches from the family members. Sobs and wails echoed off the tall church walls during the service. I stared at a large poster picture of Nick that had been placed on a stand near the front and recalled his invincible spirit and optimistic smile.

After the service, I spoke briefly with Nick's wife and her family before they ushered us to our cars to form a procession. We followed a hearse to the burial site, where Air Force personnel lowered the casket into a grave. Four airmen then raised rifles skyward and fired off a twenty-one-gun salute. I shuddered as each boom conjured images of Arid Uka screaming Allahu Akbar before squeezing the trigger.

The flight back to the UK was one of the longest and most agonizing I'd ever taken. Images of Nick's casket tortured my soul and made it impossible for me to sleep. Back home, most nights I tossed and turned for hours after being jolted awake by nightmares.

A few days after Nick's funeral, I met with my assigned counselor, David Saunders, at Lakenheath. He was a retired Army officer in his late fifties with a jovial face and kind eyes. He was a bit heavyset, partly bald, and wore wire-rimmed glasses that made him look like a high school science teacher. He spoke with a soft voice and started by asking me personal questions about myself, my family, and why I had joined the military. I told him that 9/11 had ignited a fire in my soul. I had been motivated and determined to serve my country by that tragedy. I knew that sounded cliché, but it was the truth. I had joined the military to do a job that others might not want to do. After 9/11, my friends and I had a tough time sleeping at night. I wanted to do my part to help others feel safe, so they didn't have to toss and turn in their beds like I had.

David then asked about the incident at Frankfurt and how that had impacted me. I described what had happened and explained that after 3/2, I again couldn't sleep. I kept seeing the dark man in the hoodie standing at the front of the bus. I smelled the gunpowder, heard the ear-splitting booms, saw the blood fly, and heard my friends cry out in pain. I also kept seeing the barrel of Arid Uka's gun pointed at my face. I was constantly haunted by the question of why Zachary and Nick had been killed and not me.

David sympathized and then had me again talk about what had happened. He also asked me to write it down several times in a journal. He explained that even though this exercise was difficult, revisiting the event frequently would help me process what had happened and make it easier to deal with. At first, I was skeptical, but over time I saw glimmers of hope that David's prescribed course of action might work.

He also encouraged me to learn more about PTSD and explained that it was not uncommon to feel guilty about experiencing symptoms, especially when I hadn't yet served in a combat zone. I was shocked to discover that the percentage of active military and veterans suffering from PTSD was almost twice that of the general population. Almost 90 percent of military personnel reported being exposed to at least one traumatic situation that could trigger post-traumatic stress, and most experienced three or four such events while serving.

The American Psychiatric Association's Diagnostic and Statistical Manual of Mental Disorders (DSM–5) reveals various types of mental health problems that military personnel have experienced to some degree. Most psychiatrists and medical doctors know the PTSD DSM–5 diagnostic criteria quite well. They know that individuals with PTSD often continuously allow their minds to relive the traumatic events like a tongue that keeps touching a mouth sore. This type of intrusive thinking might include vivid nightmares and frequent flashbacks.

Trauma affects everyone differently. Recalling disturbing events can be emotionally distressing, and many individuals with PTSD might avoid people, places, or things that remind them of these experiences. Whether unconsciously or intentionally, they will avoid situations that might trigger the painful thoughts. I figured that was why few of us had wanted to venture off base. Individuals with PTSD will often decline to talk about the situation that caused it with anyone except those who shared the same or similar experiences. That was definitely the case with the team. We often commented that we could only talk about what had happened with each other. Even though well-meaning, our parents, spouses, or significant others couldn't understand what we'd gone through. None of us were looking for sympathy or an easy way out of the military—just the opposite. We all wanted to go back to some semblance of normality and continue to serve. For a few, I feared that might not happen. Gunshots, uniforms, Humvees, or fighter jets screaming down a runway could be enough to curl them into a ball on the floor. For these brave souls who had sacrificed their sanity for their country, an early medical discharge might be the only option.

For me, guilt was my tormentor. My judge, jury, and executioner. Despite the best efforts of my counselor, I had trouble shaking the thought that I should have done something more to prevent the shooting. If only I'd gone with Nick when he'd asked me to join him for a smoke. If only I'd crawled out from behind my seat and leaped at the attacker. If only it had been me instead of someone else. Over time, my guilt turned to anger, and whenever I saw a bus, instead of curling into a ball, I curled my fingers into fists.

Determined to soldier on, or in my case airman on, I continued with my desk job for the next several months while meeting with my counselor every other week. Two of the guys on our team of eleven now worked for me in vehicle control as watchmen. We occasionally got together with the rest of the team to have dinner or a few beers. Some could process and deal with what had happened easier and faster than others, depending on their backgrounds. They were redeployed within a few months to Saudi Arabia or other locales while the rest of us remained on light duty and continued to see counselors.

A few more months passed before we saw Kyle in person. They finally released him from the hospital in Germany, and he came back to Lakenheath briefly to grab his gear. Given the extent of his injuries, there was little chance he'd be able to serve again, so he'd likely be medically discharged. For now, he and his wife were returning to their home in North Dakota. Before Kyle left, we had one last get together at his home in England. We sizzled burgers on a grill, drank beers, and spent one last afternoon together as a team.

I later heard that the director of the Security Forces, Brigadier General Jimmy McMillian, awarded Kyle a purple heart.

That summer, I didn't know what my future held and hoped that someday I'd be able to leave Lakenheath and serve in a combat zone. I knew that would never happen until the constant nightmares and Pavlov's Dog reactions to loud noises and sudden movements subsided. Just when I thought that was starting to happen, my PTSD flared again when I received news that Uka's trial had begun on August 14, 2011. At the opening of his trial in Frankfurt, the twenty-two-year-old terrorist from Kosovo read aloud his written statement, wherein he said he wanted "to apologize to everyone." I wanted to have sympathy for the young man. I wanted to believe his words were sincere. I wanted to forgive him, but I wasn't ready to do any of those things.

Summer faded away and fall brought cool winds, gray skies, and frequent rain. Colonel Quintas invited me to his office. He was fit and trim, with short, jet-black hair and a broad smile. He'd graduated from the Air Force Academy in 1988, flown F-111 and F-15E fighters, served as commander of Bagram Airfield in Afghanistan, and then assumed command of the 48th Fighter Squadron at Lakenheath in June 2010. Quintas asked how and I and the others on my team were doing, and I told him that most of us were still trying to cope, but the counseling and our team camaraderie were helping. Obviously, a few had moved on and deployed and others had been discharged, but the rest of us were determined to return to normal duties soon. Quintas sympathized and told me a few stories about how he and others had dealt with combat trauma at Bagram. Hearing that the base colonel had also endured several months of difficulty helped me feel less guilty and also gave me hope I could eventually serve in the field again.

Winter in England began in late October 2011 with a few breezy days, followed by sporadic gusts of frosty wind that glued the F-16s to the tarmac. Flight operations were suspended, and they put us on high alert to monitor for potential damages to buildings and equipment.

The weather cleared on a bright Saturday morning, and Colonel Quintas granted permission to allow families to gather for a Halloween celebration. The base had contracted with a vendor who brought in a massive yellow and green inflated rubber structure that resembled a haunted English castle. They set up other winter wonderland attractions on a grassy knoll and invited base personnel to the event. I was on-duty that day, patrolling with another airman named Bob. We parked our police vehicle and strolled over to the area. Bright-eyed and full of smiles, dozens of kids flocked to the castle where their parents watched them jump atop the inflated rubber.

The carnival scent of hotdogs and popcorn made my stomach growl. I glanced up as a chilled gust of wind brushed my cheek. While watching the trampoline-jumping children squeal with delight and their parents grin and wave, I noticed scraps of paper fly into the air. Then bits of grass and dirt swirled upward and formed miniature tornado plumes. I radioed my boss and recommended we temporarily suspend the celebration until the gusts subsided.

My boss hesitated but then finally agreed. My team and I played bad cops and asked the families to move away from any structures until the wind died. They groaned, complained, and eventually complied, but not in time. Several kids were still jumping and playing when a strong gale played havoc with the playground structures. The wind whistled and whined. The ropes securing the large jumping castle to the ground popped taut as the gusts sailed underneath the inflated castle and tried to make it fly. The wind finally won.

My eyes widened when the ropes broke free, and the bouncy castle bucked up and down like a wild steer at a rodeo. A few kids were flung free and thudded onto the grass. I ran over and helped dads grab crying children before the castle started tumbling end over end. Fortunately, no one was hurt beyond a few bumps and bruises, but we now had a twenty-foot-tall structure rolling toward a roadway, and potentially a runway.

Resembling a huge, inflated beach ball, the castle gained momentum and headed toward the street. I signaled Bob, and we scrambled into our police car. I gunned the engine and sped toward the out-of-control structure. Bob pointed and gasped as an airman stepped in front of the tumbling object and tried to stop it. No joy. The castle knocked the guy to the ground and bounced over him as if nothing more than a speed bump.

We pulled to a stop briefly to check on the downed airman. He was dazed but fine. I called for a medic and then climbed back into the car. I floored the gas pedal and raced after the castle. Now rolling at almost thirty miles per hour, the object had become more than an annoyance. Given its speed and weight, it was now a potential weapon.

The castle careened toward a parked government vehicle. The window sticker showed it belonged to a colonel. It smashed the windshield and then slammed onto the hood and left a crater in the middle. The vehicle's alarm blared in agony as the castle rolled onward toward a dozen more parked cars. Bob tapped me on the shoulder and pointed. He saw what I saw. If the castle got past that line of cars, it could roll out onto the flight line where dozens of aircraft were parked. Personnel were tending to the jet fighters, ensuring they were secure and tied down. If the bouncing object hit someone, it might cause serious injury.

My mind raced while I pondered our options. How could we stop a twenty-foot-tall, thirty-mile-per-hour inflated structure before it flattened airplanes and airmen on the runway? My Check Six training flashed into my head.

Three.

Escape, barricade, or fight back. It was an inflated bouncing castle. Obviously, fighting back was the only option.

Two.

Live or die? I doubted whether a kid's trampoline structure was going to kill anyone, but it could smash some planes and put some people in the hospital.

One.

We had one shot and needed to act now, before the damn thing rolled onto the runway. But how?

Mother Nature must have heard me and intervened. The wind shifted enough to roll the castle off course. It whacked into two parked cars and got wedged in between bumpers. I slammed on the brakes and skidded to a stop. Bob and I jumped out and ran toward the structure. It was bouncing up and down in the gusting wind, and I knew we only had seconds before it broke free and started rolling again.

How were we going to stop this thing?

A thought popped into my head. I reached for my belt and felt for my knife. I pulled it free and held it skyward while yelling at my partner. He glanced over, nodded, and grabbed his own knife. Together, we ran toward the castle. Just before it broke free, we jumped on top of the thing and repeatedly jabbed our knives into the rubber. The air inside shot out and mingled with the storm winds. Yelling and screaming like crazed maniacs, we slashed away. Finally, the castle lost the battle and deflated into a large yellow puddle on the ground. Gasping and tired, Bob and I fell to the ground and looked at each other. Bob grinned. I grinned back. Then he chuckled. I laughed and my eyes welled up, but this time not with sorrow. While the crazy castle had caused some damages and injuries, they had fortunately been mild. In hindsight, it was a pretty funny situation.

Bob cocked his head sideways and said, "Terrorist attack?"

I smiled back. "Had to be. A Tango obviously rigged that thing to break free and smash the colonel's car."

I imagined the next day's headlines in the base newsletter: "Wind-crazed bouncy castle destroys colonel's car before attacking a squadron of F-15s. Finally defeated by knife-wielding security personnel."

I laughed as I wondered if they'd award me and Bob a Airman's Medal for our bravery. That was the first time I'd laughed in months. It was also the first time I'd been in a stressful situation without thinking about the Frankfurt shooting. I sighed with relief as I realized I was finally ready to get back into the game.

CHAPTER 16:

THE TRIAL

By early November 2011, I had made good progress on my journey back to the old Trevor. He was the one that could laugh, have fun, and live a normal life—the one that could sleep more than a few hours at night. That all changed with one agonizing phone call. Even though I knew it was coming, it didn't lessen the blow.

Colonel Quintas spoke with an apologetic tone when he said I'd been summoned to Frankfurt to testify at Arid Uka's trial. My heart took off like an F-15 scrambling down a runway, and I almost dropped my phone. I was silent for a long moment. Quintas asked if I was okay. I lied and said I was.

That night, the nightmares returned. I stayed awake for hours, drenched in sweat. I was also ashamed. I felt like a coward who couldn't deal with his PTSD. I hadn't yet served in Afghanistan or any war zone and was mad at myself for even having PTSD.

I met with my counselor, who told me that when anger or anxiety overcame me, I should breathe deeply, open my hands, and turn my palms upward. That should help me stay calm. He helped me gather my wits enough to get on a plane and fly to Germany in October 2011.

In the Frankfurt hotel, I straightened the jacket on my civilian suit, skipped breakfast, and went down to the lobby. The German police met me there, drove me to a German higher court, and escorted me inside. A German court associate named Leon met me at the door, shook my hand, and welcomed me to Germany. He had bright eyes and a fresh face. Inside, the rectangular courtroom chamber looked like a small library without any books; about seventy-five-feet wide by one-hundred-feet long. Wood panels lined the walls. As the day's proceedings had not yet begun, it was mostly empty. A long oak desk, perpendicular to the judge's station, sat in the middle of the room. Strewn across the table were several large binders, books, and a few notebook computers. Silver microphones hung on curved metal stands fastened to the desk.

Leon glanced around the room, spotted someone, and pointed to a tall man standing in front of a table. The man turned and waved. Leon waved back. With a heavy German accent, he said, "That's him. Marcus Traut. He's the attorney especially assigned to represent you and the other surviving airmen. He's a good guy. You will like him, yes?"

I said yes, I'm sure I will. We walked to the center of the room, where Traut shook my hand. His grip was firm and confident. He appeared to be in his early forties, with short brown hair and a receding hairline. A long black robe fell to his feet, under which he wore a white shirt and a white tie. Traut explained that the German court had selected him to represent me and the others on my team who were still alive. This statement confused me until he explained that German trials differed from those in the U.S. or UK. He said that in

Germany, one attorney—in this case, him—represents the survivors, including me.

Traut pointed across the room to another attorney, Marcus Steffel, who had been selected to speak on behalf of those who could no longer speak for themselves—Airman First Class Zachary Cuddeback and Senior Airman Nick Alden. Steffel was also in his forties and had dark, curly hair and chubby cheeks. Traut pointed toward another man in a dark suit and black robe and said Jochen Weingarten would be the prosecuting attorney. He had an unshaven, almost gaunt face and wore wire-rimmed glasses. Traut then turned and nodded toward a younger woman with long dark hair. He said the court had appointed Michaela Roth to represent Arid Uka.

Traut said that during the trial, none of the attorneys could ask questions. In Germany, only the judges can do this. Also, even though the judges speak English, only German can be spoken in the courtroom and translators or attorneys whisper translations to foreigners. Traut said I should not respond until I understood the entire English version of the question asked.

I nodded and then asked if *he* would be at the trial.

Traut placed a hand on my shoulder. His eyes softened. "Yes, Arid Uka will be here today."

My jaw tightened.

Traut said the trial had been ongoing since August and would likely continue for a few more weeks. Hopefully, I should only need to attend today's session.

"Hopefully?" I said.

"It is unlikely you will need to return," Traut said. "Unless you are required to do so by the judges."

"I apologize for being nervous," I said. "This is the first time I've returned to Frankfurt since the shooting. The last time I saw Uka was the day he pointed a gun at my head."

"I understand why you might be nervous." Traut said. "There is no need to apologize."

Traut looked up as Leon waved from the across the room. Standing next to him was an older man dressed in a suit and tie. Traut motioned for Leon to bring the man over. He turned to me and asked if I'd ever met Zachary Cuddeback's father. I shook my head no. Traut said the father was here to represent his son.

Leon and the older gentleman approached. Zachary's father had white hair and several deep age lines on his forehead. I suspected that many of those had been earned over the last six months. His eyes watered as he shook my hand and introduced himself as Robert Cuddeback. He thanked me for what I'd done at the airport, and for ensuring that other fathers didn't need to endure the agony he and his wife had. I said I'd just done my job and wished I'd been able to prevent what had happened. He returned a silent nod before taking a seat in the courtroom.

A wave of guilt covered me with shame. I could tell that this ordeal was much harder on Robert Cuddeback than it was on me. I stood up tall and adjusted my tie. I needed to do my part to ensure that Zachary and Nick received the justice they deserved, and so their families could have closure. Even though the man who'd tried to kill me would be sitting a mere fifteen feet away, I was determined to do my best to stay focused, calm, and in control during the trial.

As the room filled, I did not see Lamar Conner, the American veteran who'd stood next to me at the McDonald's before Uka had been arrested. I assumed he was testifying on a different day. I took a seat on one side of the room next to Marcus Traut and my court-appointed translator.

A door opened and Arid Uka, guarded by two German police officers, walked into the room. He sat next to Michaela Roth, and the trial began. They had charged Uka with two counts of murder and three counts of attempted murder. Formal pleas do not exist in German trials, but Uka said he was not guilty because he believed the Muslim community was at war with the United States. His acts were therefore not murder or attempted murder, but nothing more than shots fired on a battlefield.

The judges called me forward and started drilling me with questions. I knew they were only doing their jobs and trying to ensure impartial proceedings, but I felt more like a defendant than a witness. Agonizing memories of Catherine's court martial in the Azores made me quaver, and for a moment, I was terrified that Arid Uka might actually be found not guilty.

The red-robed judges fired off several more tough questions and then asked me to return to my seat. Over the course of the next few hours, Uka smiled and whispered to his attorney as the judges queried other witnesses—including individuals who'd seen me race into the airport or had watched Uka try to stab me near the McDonald's. I'd been focused on Uka at the time of the incident, so I did not recognize any of them.

During the trial, the judges questioned Nick's father, James Alden, who told the court that Nick had been born in Germany when he and his wife were stationed there. Nick had become a military police airman to help people and he had been looking forward to serving in Afghanistan. James' voice turned raspy as he said that Nick had many great qualities, one of his greatest being his gentleness and desire to serve the public. James concluded by saying his family had been devastated by Nick's death.

One judge finally brought the day's session to a close. Uka rose from his seat and the German police pointed him toward an exit door. Traut thanked me for my testimony and for staying calm during the trial. He said he hoped that for me, the entire affair was now over, and that Uka would receive a guilty conviction on or about January 19. While I was glad I'd been able to mostly remain calm while the judges fired off questions, I didn't know whether I could believe Traut. I did not know if Arid Uka might receive a light sentence or be set free. If the latter were to happen, I did not know if I'd be able to refrain from chambering a round in my service weapon before firing a shot on Uka's battlefield.

CHAPTER 17:

THE REDEMPTION

After my day in court, I returned to the cold and harsh rains that besieged the Lakenheath Air Base as the Uka trial dragged on in Germany. I was wondering if it would ever end, or if the judges might give Uka a free hall pass or a slap on the wrist. Traut had assured me there was little chance of the former, but he was less certain about the latter.

In mid-January, I was called into my Chief's office. He told me to pack for another trip to Germany, only this time, my commander and a Lakenheath public affairs officer (PAO) would accompany me. Startled, I asked if they had summoned me back to court. My Chief said no, I was not being asked to testify again. Instead, I had been asked to attend an awards ceremony.

"A ceremony for what?" I asked.

"They're going to give you a medal," he said. "In Berlin."

A few days later I gathered my gear and strolled over to a building where an Air Force van idled. The three of us climbed in and they drove us to Heathrow Airport. As we approached, memories of March 2 resurfaced. I closed my eyes and tried to will them away.

We flew to Berlin on January 15, 2012, and checked in to the Hotel Adlon, right next to the U.S. Embassy and the Brandenburg Gate. That afternoon, representatives from the Federal Ministry of the Interior gave us a tour of the city. We visited the Berlin Wall, and I recalled that after World War II, they had divided Berlin into four quadrants occupied by the U.S., UK, France, and Soviet Union. By order of the Soviet Union's president, Nikita Khrushchev, the wall had been erected in 1961 to keep workers from fleeing to West German regions. The fifteen-foot-high wall, guarded by 302 watchtowers, spanned almost one hundred miles. Tens of thousands of land mines and machine guns, activated by tripwires, kept citizens from seeking freedom in West Germany. On our tour, we visited the three checkpoints, Alpha, Beta, and Charlie, where only those displaying proper papers could cross. Hundreds of people without those papers had died trying to escape until the wall came down in 1989, literally by mistake.

Apparently, Soviet government spokesperson Günter Schabowski misquoted a Russian politburo memo authorizing citizens to apply for travel visas to leave East Germany. He instead announced that anyone could leave at any time. Hundreds of thousands of East Germans immediately besieged the three checkpoints while scrambling to cross. Finally forced to relent, the guards opened the gates, and not long after, the infamous wall came down.

Standing in front of the dusty remains of Checkpoint Charlie reminded me that terrorism is not new. Warped minds have been terrorizing innocent people since the dawn of time. Those who crave power, become consumed by anger, or allow fear to rule their actions are compelled to impose their will on others. History is replete with the shameful attempts of so-called leaders who have failed to exert control over the masses. They squeeze their fists tighter to maintain their rule, but the sands of freedom always slip through.

The next morning, a German police car drove us to the Federal Ministry of the Interior, housed in a large, rectangular, off-white building. Along the way, we were told that the Ministry was the equivalent of the U.S. Department of Homeland Security and the Department of Justice combined. They employed over 50,000 people, and our award ceremony would take place in a large conference room near the entrance. Once inside the building, I recognized Lamar Conner, who was standing in a corner. I walked over, smiled, and shook his hand. He returned my smile and welcomed me back to Germany. I said thanks, but I wish I did not need to be here. He nodded and said nothing.

An hour later, after endless preparations, they asked Conner and me to stand in front of a crowd of observers and reporters who had gathered in the building. Federal Interior Minister Hans-Peter Friedrich stood from a chair and approached. He had curled dark brown hair and wore thin glasses. Addressing the crowd, Friedrich cited our exemplary courage and action, which had helped the federal police arrest the suspect. He then presented Conner and me with the Cross of the Order of Merit of the Federal Republic.

Federal Minister Friedrich turned, smiled, and thanked us for our bravery and selflessness on behalf of the public. He then said, "Your action, Mr. Conner and Staff Sergeant Brewer, was not only exemplary, it was also politically significant. The attack on the second of March 2011 was the first Islamist terrorist attack carried out in Germany. We Germans have so far been spared the anguish experienced by the American people as the result of September 11."

Recalling the events of 9/11, I swallowed hard.

Friedrich continued. "The fact that courageous individuals were able to stop the first Islamist-motivated murderer in Germany before he could harm even more people sends an important signal. This attack was aimed at the common fight of Germany and the U.S. on behalf of peace and freedom.

"As interior minister of the Federal Republic of Germany, I would like to emphasize today in a very special way our excellent transatlantic cooperation in the fight against international terrorism. I speak for the federal chancellor and the entire federal government when I say that, from the very first, we were resolved to stand with our American friends even more firmly in the hour of this attack."

Following the awards ceremony, they asked Conner and me to share our stories about what had happened on March 2, 2011. It took all the willpower I could muster to do so while keeping my voice steady. Several times I had to stop and take a sip of water before continuing.

Members of the media then raised hands so they could ask us questions. One reporter, in accented English, said, "Mr. Conner, congratulations on your well-deserved award. You did not hesitate to pursue the attacker as he fled the military bus at Frankfurt Airport on the second of March 2011. You shouted to warn passersby, gave the alarm, and were instrumental in helping the federal police make the arrest. What was going through your head at the time?"

Conner cleared his throat. "For me, the most important thing was to protect the other people nearby. There wasn't much time to think. I just reacted."

Another reporter jumped in. "You knew that the attacker had a gun and a knife. Weren't you afraid that he might turn on you with these weapons as you pursued him?"

Conner nodded. "Sure, I was afraid, but I was able to control my fear. The worst moment came after I had warned the passersby, when the attacker turned around to face me. But at the same time, he saw that the police had spotted him. Then he turned back around and kept running."

Conner, who was now in his early fifties, had served as a U.S. Army sergeant in Germany and remained there after retiring. He'd gotten a job at the airport and had been off duty when he'd heard the shots fired on our Air Force bus. He then saw Uka run off the bus with a gun in his hand. Military instinct kicked in and he gave chase.

"I just fell in behind him," Conner said, "and followed him while warning passersby."

Another reporter fired off a question. "The suspect in this first Islamist terrorist act carried out on German soil is now on trial. What kind of sentence are you hoping for?"

Conner's faced hardened. "I hope he gets a life sentence. I would like to see him get two life sentences, as is standard procedure in some other countries, and I hope the attempted murder of the three other troops is taken into account during sentencing."

A reporter in the back raised their hand and leveled a question at me. "Staff Sergeant Brewer...you were not wounded in the attack at Frankfurt Airport on March 2, 2011, apparently because the attacker's weapon jammed. He had aimed directly at you, after killing two of your fellow airmen and seriously wounding two others. That must have been a traumatic experience for you. How are you coping with it today? Are you even more aware of what's going on around you now than before the attack?"

My throat went dry. I was silent for a moment before answering. "You can say I'm coping pretty well with it," I lied. Then I spoke the truth. "I would definitely say my training in the past has prepared me for such an event and has helped me in the aftermath of the attack."

The same reporter continued. "You didn't hesitate to pursue the attacker after he fled, you alerted federal police at the airport so that they were able to catch the attacker, and you informed Mr. Conner, who also received an award here today, of the victims at the troop bus so that help could be called. How did you have the presence of mind to do all that after having escaped death so narrowly yourself?"

I blew out a long breath. "I have to say again that goes back to my training that I've had in the past...all these steps, things that we were taught to do in case of an event of law enforcement or an attack. And the training definitely kicked in and helped."

The media asked a few more questions before the crowd dispersed. On our ride back to the Berlin Airport, beaming with excitement, our Lakenheath PAO offered details about the medal I'd received. He said German Federal President Theodor Heuss had created the Order of Merit of the Federal Republic of Germany in 1951. It's the highest tribute the Federal Republic of Germany can pay to someone for their service to the German nation. They award the Order of Merit to Germans or foreigners for outstanding economic, political, social, intellectual, or philanthropic achievements. In my case, they considered it social in that German citizens had potentially been protected from harm.

During the return flight from Berlin to the UK, I couldn't help but have mixed emotions. I was proud to have received such a high honor, but I was also deeply saddened by the events that had led to the award being issued. I had only accepted to honor the memory of Nick and Zachary.

The following month, on February 10, 2012, while cradling a cup of coffee, I picked up a copy of the *Stars and Stripes*. My mouth fell open. The headline read that Arid Uka had been convicted of two counts of murder and three counts of attempted murder. German Judge Thomas Sagebiel had ruled that Uka's actions warranted "particularly severe guilt." He said Uka had turned our Air Force bus into a "deadly tunnel." He then cited the premeditated nature of the ambush on our team, the way he had shot Zachary and Nick, and the severity of the injuries he had inflicted on Kevin and Kyle as reasons for Uka being ineligible for parole in fifteen years.

I was sick to my stomach when I read that Uka, while wearing green trousers, a black jumper, and a brown hooded top, appeared relaxed during the proceedings. After the judges announced the conviction, he simply smiled and chatted with his attorney, as if he were now a celebrity. Nick Alden's brother, Joe, had been in the courtroom during the ruling. Later, when the press asked his opinion about the verdict, he said, "I'm satisfied. I'm at peace. There's a huge weight off our shoulders. I think justice has been served. I think he got what he deserved, and I think the court did a great job. I wish there was more they could do, but he got the maximum."

I also wish there had been more they could have done, but I agree with Joe. At least Uka got the maximum penalty and will spend the rest of his life behind bars. Someday I hope to forgive, but I will never forget.

CHAPTER 18

THE FUTURE

Coincidentally, on the same day Arid Uka was sentenced to life in prison, the Air Force gave me another medal. I read about the trial's conclusion in the morning, and Colonel Quintas asked me to attend an awards ceremony that afternoon. I was presented with the Airman's Medal. The award is the highest issued by the U.S. Air Force for a heroic act involving voluntary risk of one's life in a non-combat situation. Although I did not at all feel like a hero, the Air Force had presented me with the medal for my actions at the Frankfurt Airport. A senior master sergeant also received the Airman's Medal for acts of courage while serving in Afghanistan, and a few members of the team received medals for their part in the Frankfurt incident.

I was introduced to the Senior Master Sergeant, and we shook hands before preparing for the ceremony. I again could not help but be honored, but I also could not dispel the anguish, anger, and strong desire to reverse the events that had qualified me for the medal.

Those feelings subsided when I saw my parents walk through the door and enter the auditorium. They had flown out from the U.S. to attend the ceremony, and both beamed when they spotted me. I walked over, gave them a hug, and escorted them to front row seats reserved for family. I then walked onto the stage and stood next to the other two awardees. We popped to attention when four-star General Norton Schwartz, the nineteenth chief of staff of the Air Force, strode through the door. He smiled as he greeted Colonel Quintas and several other base officers. Schwartz was a moderately tall man who stood erect. He had graying hair and a narrow face. He was not bulky but carried a runner's physique. I suspected that even at his age, he probably still jogged several miles per day and hit the gym frequently. I knew Schwartz had grown up in New Jersey as the son of a typewriter salesperson. He'd graduated from the U.S. Air Force Academy and flew combat aircraft and helicopters during Desert Storm. I recalled that on 9/11, Schwartz had been a lieutenant general and a commander of the Alaskan Command, under the North American Aerospace Defense Command (NORAD). Korean Air Flight 85, en route to Anchorage Airport, had suddenly transmitted the international hijack transponder code. Believing that terrorists had taken over the plane, and it might therefore try to crash into a target, Schwartz had ordered Air Force fighters to escort the plane to a Canadian airport. Once the plane landed, they discovered that the pilots had sent the hijack code in error. Many believe the general's quick thinking and decisive actions during that event eventually led to his promotion to chief of staff.

Schwartz walked onto the stage, smiled, and shook our hands while taking a moment to greet all three of us. He walked to the podium, silenced the attendees, and started the ceremony. The Senior Master Sergeant and I were the first to receive medals. General

Scwartz handed me a small box with my medal inside and then shook my hand. Cameras flashed and my chest tightened as I recalled the events that had led to this moment. I again saw the angry face of Arid Uka standing at the front of the bus and heard Senior Airman Ortiz scream. I clenched my jaw and forced a smile as the photographers snapped pictures.

Over the next few days, I spent time with my parents, giving them a tour of the base, my home in Beck Row, and the surrounding English countryside. I bid them farewell and resumed my duties on the base. I received a brief text from Rachel congratulating me for my medal. She'd heard about it through Air Force news channels. We hadn't been able to stay in touch very often, given our respective duties and time zone differences, and we'd both reluctantly concluded that keeping a long-distance relationship alive had been more difficult than we'd expected.

News articles and television reports about the incident and Arid Uka's conviction subsided, but a few details emerged that I had not previously been aware of. I learned that Uka had apparently been sexually abused when he was only six years old. If true, this may have been why scenes showing Afghan women being raped by U.S. soldiers in the movie *Redacted* had compelled him to act. During his conviction proceedings, Uka told the court, "On March 2, I killed two people and opened fire on three others. Today I can't understand myself, how I could have acted this way." Referring to the film *Redacted*, he said he had been influenced by lies and propaganda after seeing the movie on YouTube.

Hollywood producers and media executives often hide behind the U.S. First Amendment. They claim to have the right to say and depict anything they want, regardless of any unintended consequences. America's First Amendment rights are designed to protect our freedom of religion, assembly, and speech, but they are not without limits. We do not have the right to say anything we want, whenever we want, to whomever we want, regardless of the serious harm we might cause others. Free speech is one of our most cherished civil liberties and should be protected with zeal. I may not always agree with what someone thinks or says, but as a member of the military, I will defend, to the death, their right to say it.

However, freedom of speech can sometimes come into conflict with other liberties and rights. U.S. courts have often had to determine what constitutes the limits of free speech by applying the basic principle of whether something spoken, posted, or printed can cause a "clear and present danger" to U.S. citizens. The famous *Schenck v. United States* case set this basic principle in stone during World War I. The authorities arrested antiwar activist Charles Schenck for distributing leaflets to prospective Army draftees. In print, he encouraged men to protest the war by ignoring their draft notices. Attorneys representing the United States claimed that Schenck's actions threatened national security, and the court agreed. The case ruling established that free speech would not be protected if an individual's written or uttered words caused a clear and present danger to United States security.

During World War I, we were at war with the Germans. Today, along with Germany as our ally, we are at war with radical terrorists. They frequently prey upon men and women like Arid Uka. They seek those with ethnic backgrounds, religious beliefs, or traumatic childhoods that might be easy prey. They use social media platforms, books, religious gatherings, or movies to twist minds and brainwash the innocent. Ever since 9/11, and during the subsequent wars in Iraq and Afghanistan, most Americans have become well informed about terrorism and the cunning tactics employed by the Taliban, al-Qaeda, and other factions. While one can argue that a film like *Redacted* was not solely responsible for Arid Uka's actions, should its producers be held harmless? Should they be allowed to cite First Amendment rights as an excuse to film scenes of American soldiers raping Afghan women that any reasonable person might assume could be used by terrorist groups to subvert or radicalize followers? Should they be held responsible, at least in part, for pushing Arid Uka toward the cliff that sent him headlong toward an Air Force bus?

I don't know the answers to these questions. But I do believe that had the rape scene in *Redacted* been redacted, Uka might not have stolen his brother's gun. He might not have shoved it into his backpack and then hid in the shadows at the Frankfurt Airport. He might not have waited for hours until he spotted our team and saw our camo bags and short hair. He might not have followed close behind as Zachary Cuddeback led us toward the blue-gray bus. He might not have approached Nick Alden and asked for a cigarette. He might not have shot Nick and then stormed onto the bus. He might not have killed Zachery and seriously wounded Kyle Ritter and Kevin Ortiz. He might not have pointed that Browning 9mm at my head and clicked the trigger. Twice.

More than a decade has passed since March 2, 2011, and I'm still a proud member of the United States Air Force. I'm a master sergeant now, and for many years I have traveled the globe while speaking to Air Force personnel at dozens of bases. Regardless of how difficult it has been for me to relive the terror in Frankfurt, I continue to frequently retell the story. My goal is not to seek glory or recognition. It is not to gain sympathy or admiration. My motivation has only been to inform and instruct so that others can hopefully avoid the tragic events our team endured at the Frankfurt Airport.

I recall one speaking engagement in 2018 at Eielson Air Force Base in Alaska. After the event, while visiting with base personnel, an airman approached. He was a cheerful young man with peach fuzz cheeks and eager eyes. He thanked me for my talk and said that I'd helped him make a difficult decision. When I inquired, he said that he hadn't yet decided on his career choice for the Air Force and had been wavering about what to do. When he heard me talk about serving in Security Forces to ensure the safety of others, all doubts vanished. He had decided to become an Air Force cop. I smiled, shook his hand, and wished him the best. A warm feeling filled my chest. I'd spent my career doing my best to fulfill my mission to protect others. By helping one airman move beyond indecision or fear to also help protect others, I'd been given the opportunity to pass the baton forward.

I've also been given the opportunity to speak at various civilian events, and I've done my best to encourage young adults to serve their country. Whether it's in the Peace Corps, the military, or something similar, I believe it can help educate, motivate, and shape them into the future leaders our country needs. While struggling through boot camp and Security Forces training, I harbored some doubts about whether I'd made the right decision, but today I'm glad I stuck with it. The Air Force taught me valuable lessons about tolerance, respect, and compassion. I learned to tolerate and even admire others from different cultures and lands. I learned to respect differing opinions and viewpoints rather than remain stubborn or dismissive. And I learned to have compassion and empathy for those less fortunate or in pain.

Given our respective schedules, it's not been easy to keep in touch with Rachel. While it proved impossible to keep our long-distance romantic relationship going, we're still close friends. It's also been a challenge to keep in touch with my superiors or my team from the Frankfurt shooting, but we've all done our best. I occasionally connect via social networks with Nick Alden's family and Zachery Cuddeback's parents to check in.

I keep in contact with Lamar Conner from Germany and would like to one day visit Ramstein to participate in a 5K run to honor Zachary. Colonel Quintas became the deputy director for the Bureau of Political-Military Affairs in July 2015 and then retired in 2017 as a major general.

I struggled for many years to resume my full duties and again handle firearms. I never imagined that going to a range for target practice would be so hard. I finally moved beyond my trepidation enough to win the gold medal in the 2019 prone air rifle competition at Nellis Air Force Base. It was only an air rifle, but it was a start.

My message to those who may be suffering in silence is to get the help you need. Traumatic events can make it seem as if there is no resolution or end to the pain. I have sought counseling and found peace from doing so. Your mental health far outweighs almost anything else. Get the help you need while you still can.

My heart goes out to the families of those who were killed and those who were there with me that fateful day. I have yet to serve in Afghanistan, but I have served in other deployment areas. Many of my friends who did serve there were disheartened when the U.S. abruptly withdrew all troops in 2021. Several of them, while sitting in wheelchairs, watched in dismay as the Taliban recaptured cities that U.S. and Allied troops had won at grave cost. As I stood beside them and placed an understanding palm on their shoulders, I recalled 9/11 and the conviction I'd felt to serve my country and prevent a similar tragedy from happening again. I have no control over the Taliban, al-Qaeda, or other terrorist groups that continue to preach hatred and revenge. I can't stop them from brainwashing and subverting young men like Arid Uka. I can't prevent them from harming their own people or imposing harsh and undeserved punishments on women. But should they threaten my family, my friends, or my country, I stand ready to protect and defend.